Anglo Indian

Indian Outfits & Establishments

Practical Guide for Persons to Reside in India

Anglo Indian

Indian Outfits & Establishments
Practical Guide for Persons to Reside in India

ISBN/EAN: 9783337062323

Printed in Europe, USA, Canada, Australia, Japan

Cover: Foto ©ninafisch / pixelio.de

More available books at **www.hansebooks.com**

Indian Outfits & Establishments.

PRACTICAL GUIDE FOR PERSONS ABOUT TO
RESIDE IN INDIA;

DETAILING THE ARTICLES WHICH SHOULD BE TAKEN OUT,
AND THE REQUIREMENTS OF HOME LIFE AND
MANAGEMENT THERE.

By AN ANGLO-INDIAN.

London:
L. UPCOTT GILL, 170, STRAND, W.C.

1882.

PREFACE.

This book, compiled from articles which have been recently inserted in the columns of *The Bazaar*, will, it is hoped, be found of considerable service to English people, more especially young married couples, going to India for the first time. Though there are books already published on the subject of housekeeping in India, still, as numerous questions are constantly appearing in various papers asking for information respecting Indian life, it is only reasonable to suppose that a book, treating in detail of outfits, voyage and necessaries required for it, railway travelling, bungalow choosing, furnishing, management of native servants and their duties, the kitchen and recipes for various dishes, the garden and its produce, the stable and general treatment of live stock, combined with hints and suggestions on the manner of living and social customs, will help to supply an acknowledged want, and so be of use to those contemplating a sojourn in India.

ANGLO-INDIAN.

ERRATUM

Since the first portion of this book was printed, the Peninsular and Oriental Company have made an alteration in the sailing of their boats, which do not now call at Southampton. They leave Gravesend for Bombay every Wednesday, and for Calcutta every alternate Wednesday.

INDIAN
Outfits and Establishments.

CHAPTER I.

CHOICE OF ROUTE—PACKING—BAGGAGE.

The Peninsular and Oriental Company's Steamers—Overland Routes—The Bombay, Anchor, and other lines—Packing—Disposal of Baggage—The Indian Parcels Post.

HAVING determined on proceeding to India, the intending traveller's first consideration will naturally be the means of getting there. Accordingly I begin with the dry, but necessary details for affording a choice of route.

Of routes by the P. and O. Company's steamers the longest is that *viâ* Southampton; the shortest, as far as the sea voyage is concerned, that through Italy to Brindisi. The former, *viâ* Southampton, runs as follows :

Sail by steamer from Southampton on Wednesday, about 2 p.m., and take the Suez Canal for Bombay, touching at Gibraltar and Malta. Port Said is reached about four days from Malta, the Canal entered, and Suez gained. Bombay passengers are required to change steamers here every alternate week. Then comes the most trying portion of the voyage—through the Red Sea to Aden, where the steamers usually coal. After seven days more Bombay is reached. The voyage by this route occupies about twenty-eight days. The weight of baggage allowed on board free of charge is 336lb. first class, and 168lb. for children and servants; excess of baggage is charged at the rate of £1 per cwt. Passengers who prefer embarking at Brindisi can have their baggage conveyed from Southampton by the P. and O. steamers at the same rates—*i.e.*, 336lb. free of charge and payment on excess—joining the boat themselves at Alexandria, which port they will have reached *viâ* Paris. Thus: Dover to Calais by steamer, to Paris by rail, Maçon and Turin by rail (*viâ* Mont Cenis) to Brindisi, and from Brindisi to Alexandria by steamer. The time occupied is six days—three to Brindisi and three more to Alexandria. The fare, through ticket from London to Paris and Brindisi, by the South Eastern or London, Chatham, and Dover Company, is £11 17s. first class, or £8 13s. second class; by the Brighton Company £10 13s. first, or £7 13s. second class. By way of Venice the fare is rather less expensive. Passengers proceeding to either Alexandria or Suez can forward their luggage by steamer from Southampton. Between London and Paris on the Dover and Folkestone route charges are made on the excess carried over 56lbs., that amount being allowed free, and the same remark applies to the Newhaven and Dieppe route; 66lb. are allowed in France to first and second class passengers, but in Italy no allowance is made, and the charge from Modane to Brindisi is 3s. 6d. per 20lb.

Besides the P. and O. mail steamers to Bombay and China (*viâ* Canal), which leave London (Victoria Docks) every alternate Saturday, and Southampton every Wednesday, there are the following lines:

The Bombay Anchor Line, from Liverpool direct (*viâ* Suez Canal), sailings, which are every fortnight, being advertised at least a month in advance. First class 50 guineas; no other class carried.

The Clan Line, Liverpool to Bombay (*viâ* Canal), every fortnight, advertised. First class, 40 guineas; no other class.

The Hall Line, Liverpool to Bombay (*viâ* Suez Canal), calling at Malta every fortnight. First class only, fare 50 guineas.

Calcutta Star Line, from Liverpool (*viâ* Suez Canal), landing passengers at Colombo, and embarking passengers, *viâ* Naples, at Suez.

The Rubatino Line, from Genoa and Naples, for Bombay. Average passage eighteen days. Fares, first class, £50; second class £34. Sailings advertised.

There are various other lines; but whichever be selected care should be taken to write for information respecting fares, luggage, regulations, &c. If an overland route be chosen, it will be seen that but little luggage is allowed free of charge. Since, however, heavy baggage can be otherwise forwarded, this need not prove an obstacle. Unless unusual stoppages are made *en route*, the journey does not occupy many days, and a large-sized square-mouth bag will hold a good many necessaries. If a trunk be taken, it should not be more than, say, 2ft. 6in. in length, 1ft. 6in. wide, and 1ft. 4in. deep. This, with a hand-bag, should be quite enough for night and toilet requisites, including soap and towels, Eau de Cologne, a flask of brandy in case of illness, smelling salts, a needle book with working necessaries, writing materials, and any odds and ends required; a warm shawl and waterproof cloak, these strapped neatly together, and a good sized umbrella, slipped into the bundle, should be also taken. If I were going out again, rather than travel overland, I should prefer the long sea route, as thereby much trouble is saved. You settle yourself down once for all for the whole voyage. But then, I like the sea, am never troubled with that dreadful enemy, sea sickness, and never feel better than when on board ship. For those who are bad sailors and dread the longer period at sea, the overland route is better; and even more land travelling than I have described can be done by going by rail across Egypt to Suez, and joining the steamer there. Only avoid having much luggage—cut it down as much as possible, or you will find it a grievous nuisance and a considerable expense.

Closely associated with the method of conveyance is the arrangement and disposal of Baggage, and this, again, involves the consideration of Packing.

Married couples taking out linen, glass, china, and other household things should send on heavy luggage of this description, *viâ* Suez Canal, beforehand, taking charge of it on arrival at the port of destination.

All china and glass should be packed together. This is best left to the firm from whom the goods are purchased, as they thoroughly understand the packing of brittle ware for a sea voyage, and will perform it far better than could be done by the purchasers. To facilitate the business, it will be well to buy as much as possible at one large house, or else at a co-operative store, if you happen to be a member. I should prefer buying of some firms which allow discount to holders of co-operative tickets, and letting them forward the goods according to directions.

With regard to personal baggage—by which I mean all you will take with you, either by overland route or troop-ship—you will require two air-tight tin cases of similar size enclosed in wooden cases; these will cost you, including inner and outside cases, sunk handles, lock and key, hinges, &c., from 60s. upwards for the size 30in. by 24in. by 12in. (regulation size), and more, of course, for larger ones. If clamped with iron the cost will be 2s. 6d. additional.

It has become necessary to have sunk handles, as the regulations for baggage carried by troop-ships are more strict than formerly (see regulations quoted). These wooden tin-lined cases will not be wanted until arrival, and they can therefore be soldered down. A smaller box should be packed with a change of clothing for wear as the weather becomes hot, and should be marked as directed below. This can be tin-lined or not, as fancy dictates, but must not be soldered down. I may here observe, *en passant*, that all these tin cases become useful afterwards as store cases.

Besides the heavy baggage you will want two portmanteaus or bullock trunks, regulation size, for use on the voyage—one in the cabin with you, and one in the "Present Use" Baggage Room. These will cost, if tin-lined, from 56s. to 62s. You can get the regulation size trunks and boxes at the Army and Navy Co-operative stores, or of the army outfitters, or shipping agents. You should provide yourself also with a fair-sized square-mouthed bag for cabin use (you will find it invaluable), and a clothes bag for soiled linen, with lock and key.

Your heavy baggage you should send on to the port of embarkation at least six days before the date of sailing, to the care of some agent, who will see it properly put on board. Your cabin (personal) baggage you will bring with you.

Baggage in a troop-ship is divided into three classes: "Baggage Room," *i.e.*, heavy baggage, which is not available during the voyage; "Present Use Baggage Room," which can be got at every day at a stated hour; and "Cabin" articles, those so marked being allowed in the cabins. Each officer or lady is allowed two medium sized portmanteaus as cabin baggage, subject to rules respecting size, the regulation dimensions for trunks being 36in. long, 15in. wide, and 14in. deep. Printed labels (free of charge) can be obtained from the Quartermaster-General's Office at Portsmouth, Queenstown, and Bombay, or from Curtiss and Sons, Portsmouth, agents, who are always ready to afford any possible information either to the outward or homeward bound.

The trunk containing light clothing should be marked with a blue label, "Change of clothing required at Suez, Baggage Room"—(all the labels are of different colours—white for "Baggage Room," green for "Present Use Baggage Room," yellow for "Cabin," and so on), as in the Red Sea light clothing is nearly always wanted; and in the same way thick clothing should be marked accordingly on the homeward voyage. Boxes so marked will be stowed near the door of the "Baggage Room," and will be got out soon after leaving Suez or Port Said.

It may be well to give some of the principal regulations respecting military baggage, as it is not always easy to obtain this information when required.

G. O. 131.—*Embarkations—Regimental Baggage.*

1. All military baggage must be carried in rectangular boxes, to be made in accordance with patterns which have been approved and deposited in the pattern room at the Royal Army Clothing Factory, Pimlico.

2. The boxes are four in number, of the following dimensions, outside measurement :

   No. 1. 3ft. 6in. by 2ft. 2in. by 2ft.=15 cubic feet, or 3cwt. of baggage.

   No. 2. 3ft. 4in. by 1ft. 10in. by 1ft. 8in.=10 cubic feet, or 2cwt. of baggage.

   No 3. 2ft. 6in. by 2ft. 10in. by 1ft.=5 cubic feet, or 1cwt. of baggage.

   No. 4. 2ft. 2in. by 1ft. 2in. by 1ft.=2½ cubic feet, or ½cwt. of baggage.

3. No baggage will be accepted for shipment with troops embarking which does not conform to this regulation. Casks, vats, crates, hampers, and similar packages are altogether prohibited, as also are padlocks, cording, cleats for rope, handles, and all projections, as they cause loss of stowage room.

4. The following will be embarked as exceptions to the dimensions authorised :

Arm chests.	Valise for officers' bedding.
Lace chests.	Officers' tubs.
Tool chests.	Bullock trunks.
Forge.	Portmanteaus.
Officers' bedsteads.	Tin uniform cases.

Musical instrument cases.

The cubic measurement of each package to be marked in paint outside.

5. Cases at present in possession of officers may be retained if approved by the commanding officer, and marked with the number of the nearest equivalent pattern, but not to exceed 15 cubic feet. New cases, when required, must be according to the regulation.

6. Each article must have distinctly painted upon it, in front, the name and rank of the owner, or department of the corps to which it belongs, and on the top the nature of the contents, such as "personal baggage," and on each end the size, number 1, 2, 3, or 4.

7. Two articles of baggage for each officer will be allowed as cabin baggage; these are not to exceed the size and shape of the regulation box No. 3, and are to be included in the officer's total allowance of baggage.

When proceeding by sea, if their passage is provided at the public expense, officers' families are allowed the following additional baggage :

Regt. Cwt.
Each officer's wife with children under 14 years 6
Each officer's son over 14 and under 16 .... ½
Each officer's daughter, unmarried, over 14 .... ½

The weight of luggage each officer is allowed depends on his rank, and can easily be ascertained.

Bed linen is provided in the troop-ships for military officers and their families. Towels for washing are not provided.

This part of the subject would be incomplete without some mention of the Indian Parcels Post, by which things omitted in the outfit may be afterwards supplied, or household stores and stocks of clothing from time to time replenished.

The Indian Parcels Post is not connected in any way with the British Post Office, but is an arrangement between the P. and O. Steam Navigation Company and the Indian Post Office. Parcels are received by the company for delivery at any post town or in any district in India or Ceylon, at the rate of 1s. per pound or fraction of a pound. This charge covers conveyance from London to the Indian or Ceylon address (but does not include the duty), and it may be either prepaid or paid on delivery. The parcels must be forwarded to the company's office, 122, Leadenhall-street, E.C., or to their branch office, 25, Cockspur-street, London, S.W., by two o'clock p.m. on Monday in any week, with, of course, the address very legibly written, and the words "to be forwarded by Indian Parcel Post" marked in a conspicuous place. If sent by post to London they will need two wrappers, the inner bearing the Indian address, first given, and the outer the address of the company. Every package must be accompanied by a letter of advice to the company, stating the name and address on it, the nature and value of the contents, for Custom House clearance, and also whether it is to be prepaid or paid on delivery. If to be prepaid a cheque or P.O.O. must be enclosed in the letter, payable to Mr. A. M. Bethune, secretary, or, when sent to Cockspur-street, to Mr. F. H. Firth, agent. Parcels sent by this conveyance must not exceed 50lb. in weight or 2ft. by 1ft. by 1ft. in measurement, nor be of more than £50 in value. They should be entirely closed, and articles liable to suffer from crushing should be packed in a strong wooden case, which may, if necessary, be lined with tin for extra safety. Packages not in wood, if measuring one cubic foot and upwards, must have an outer covering of stout canvas. On goods so sent insurance can be effected, but it must in all cases be prepaid at the rate of 1s. up to £3 value, 2s. 6d. up to £10, 5s. up to £20, 7s. 6d. up to £30, 10s. up to £40, and 12s. 6d. up to £50. Packages of a fragile description, or containing liquids or damaging or dangerous articles are not received.

These directions may be found in the Post Office Quarterly Guide, but as such a book is not always at hand I have enumerated the most important regulations. Many of my friends who have parcels sent out in this way receive them quite safely, and find it far cheaper than to send for odds and ends to Bombay or Calcutta, and have to pay perhaps treble the value of the articles.

CHAPTER II.

OUTFIT FOR LADIES.

General Remarks—Linen—Dresses—Miscellaneous Requisites—Work for the Durzee (Tailor)—Boots and Shoes.

A LARGE outfit is not now a *sine quâ non*, as it was years ago, when the parcel post did not exist, and carriage was very expensive. It is no longer necessary to burden yourself with many dresses, many bonnets, hats, boots and shoes, &c., because such things as these can be sent out from home by any kind friend or trustworthy outfitter. I have a relative now in India who, whenever she wants them, has boots and shoes, hats, jackets, and dresses, sent out to her. I do not advise that you should start on this plan at once, for that would be extravagant. Enough at starting should be taken for a year, or even two years; for in India fashions do not succeed each other so rapidly as at home, and even in last year's bonnet or hat you will not feel yourself *démodé*.

Personal and house linen—the latter if you are married, and going out to settle down—you must certainly take, and sufficient to last you for some years, which, with care, it may easily be made to do. Also things for ornamenting your house, little trifles, which here cost a mere song, but out there you will not get "for love or money." To this point I shall refer in a future chapter. What I have to consider now is your personal outfit.

It may be concluded, that the lists commonly given are, as a rule, extravagant and too extensive, and may safely be cut down by nearly one half. The following will be found enough for any ordinary lady's wants. Prices I have not given; only the kind of articles required and the number of each. With regard to linen, two kinds should be taken; one very thin for hot weather wear, and the other of thicker texture for the colder season. I may point out, *en passant*, that your linen should not be trimmed with work; the washerman (*dhobie*) is not like Phil Robinson's punkah coolie—"a thing of dark imaginings"; but he is a creature with rough hands, and on dainty laces and trimmings works his sweet will; he has apparently a malicious pleasure in tearing off buttons and strings, and at the very first wash reducing handsome linen into untidy dilapidated garments. Do not regard, therefore, the rather plain look of your underclothing; dispense with the ornamental part of it, and you will be a gainer in pocket, to say nothing of your time being less taken up with replacing torn work and lace.

Now for your list. Should your wants be greater, add to it; and, on the other hand, subtract from it if you find the money put aside for the purpose of outfit does not "run to it."

- One dozen cotton chemises, thin; one dozen cotton chemises, thicker.
- One dozen cotton nightdresses, thin; one dozen cotton nightdresses, usual thickness.
- One dozen pairs of cotton drawers, thin; one dozen pairs of cotton drawers, thicker.
- Six vests of flannel, or of silk if preferred; the kind known as Indian gauze.
- Six white petticoats, long, for evening wear, flounced, with bodices; six shorter, and tucked, with bodices also.
- Four muslin petticoats, with trains to fasten on; these may have lace edgings for best evening wear, and laced trimmed bodices.
- Six white flannel petticoats; two red flannel petticoats; two crochet, either red or red and white.
- One flannel wrapper (coloured).
- Two short dressing jackets of some white washing material, cambric or longcloth, frilled.
- Two pairs of corsets, with extra cases to wash; one pair of evening corsets, with case.
- Twelve pairs of fine white thread stockings, not open work, but either embroidered in colour or plain white silk; twelve pairs of stockings (coloured), to match the dresses you are taking out; six pairs spun silk, black; six pairs warm (coloured), for cold weather use.
- Three dozen handkerchiefs, plain, hemstitched, initialled; one dozen trimmed with lace (you can buy these and trim them yourself); six best, either worked or lace, for evening use.
- Four pairs of long black mittens; four pairs of long white mittens.

One dozen pairs of kid gloves; six pairs of dogskin for riding.
One dozen pairs of thread or silk gloves for matching dresses.
Of collars, cuffs, frills, and the like, you must take a good stock.

The list given of linen is really sufficient for an ordinary outfit, and certainly should not cost more than £40, or, at the most, £50. In order to keep it within limits many of the things may be made at home, provided, of course, that time is not an object. Handwork is, undoubtedly, far preferable to machine work for linen, especially where it is destined to go through rough usage. But, though you may stipulate in giving out the material that handwork alone is to be employed, your orders, unless you look to it well, are likely to be disobeyed.

With regard to dress, some of the most serviceable materials are thin woollen or cloth, which are adapted for the cold weather; plain white washing calico or linen for morning wear in the hot weather; uncrushable net, gauze, or lace for evening wear, with silk slips, made body and skirt in one, to wear under them; one good black silk made with square and high body, and one or two afternoon dresses, mixtures of silk and cashmere, or tussore; some loose morning wrappers of washing materials, and one or two tea gowns of some patterned material now fashionable. Also a cloth habit, and two white washing ones; these are not expensive and exceedingly comfortable; they should not be made quite tight, but skirts and coat bodies (half fitting) separate. I found mine more useful than I can express. Piqué was the material I had one made of, thin hunting cord the other.

A dozen dresses are quite as many as you will require, it being a great mistake to take out too many, for they spoil in lying by, and you are apt to be tired of them before they are worn out. Suppose you divide your dresses somewhat after this fashion: Two plain white washing morning dresses; two loose wrappers, white washing materials. These being plain white, you can always vary them by wearing different coloured bows and bands with them. Two costumes for afternoons, of either tussore, cashmere, merino, or any other material, not too heavy, which may happen to be in fashion.

You will have hats to match these dresses, and jackets, mantles, or capes, as may be the most worn when buying. One cloth costume for cold weather wear, one ulster dress, not too thick, for wet weather and travelling; this you should have waterproofed. Do not take out velvet or velveteen if you can avoid it, as there are various insects which revel in velvet of any kind; you would have to keep it always in tin, and, notwithstanding all precautions, you would very likely find the nap eaten off in places when you took it out.

Let your black silk dress be really a good one, and I should advise, as well as two bodices, two skirts also, one of them *trotteuse* — in fact you should be able to make two costumes out of one dress. Your evening dresses you will be able to alter with the occasional addition of little extras, such as flowers, ribbons, and so on. If you can afford a lace dress (I should prefer it of white), so much the better; it will outlast many other evening dresses, and lace, even if not of an expensive kind, is always useful, and can be made up over and over again on different coloured slips. For a ball dress in India it answers better than any other material. When dirty, if you cannot wash it yourself, and there is no one in the station who can, you can send it home by post to be cleaned, and wear it again, looking quite fresh and new. You can allow yourself one good dinner dress of silk and satin, or some pretty fashionable material. Satin would be the most serviceable, black, nicely trimmed; and then with your two loose white wrappers and two of warmer material for wear in the colder weather, I think you will have enough in the way of dresses. Now let me sum them up:

> Two plain white dresses (washing).
> Two afternoon dresses (regular costumes).
> One black silk, with two skirts and two bodices.
> One cloth costume (cold weather wear).
> One ulster dress (waterproof).
> Two evening dresses (for ordinary wear, with bodies and slips).
> One lace ditto (ball dress).
> One dinner dress (full toilette).
> One dinner dress (demi toilette).
> Total, twelve dresses (besides four wrappers).

You can take out some materials unmade, with everything necessary for making them up prettily; but of these I should not advise your taking more than two or three. This is an age of change; new materials are so constantly being introduced that you may just as well send home for the most recent description of stuff as make a fresh dress up from a material worn in England when you left, perhaps two or three years before. White washing extra lengths you may take, of course; plain white can never look out of fashion or otherwise than in good taste.

Have all dresses, not washing, made with dress protectors, which you can get at any good outfitter's.

Now, having disposed of the dresses, let me give you a list of some necessary extras: A soft felt hat for travelling, waterproof—it should match your ulster dress; another to match your cloth, a shady hat, and one black bonnet, which you can vary with different flowers or ribbons. Bonnets are little worn in India; they are no protection against the sun, and one will be sufficient, for you can have hats or bonnets sent from home, or shapes, if you prefer, as some people do, to make up your own, and you will have bonnets or hats to match your two afternoon dresses.

A riding hat, a pith hat, an extra waterproof cloak to throw on, not tight fitting like an ulster, will be required; a handsome opera cloak; a loose hood lined with flannel for night travelling, or on board ship; one black parasol edged with lace, and one of some other kind. Two umbrellas, one of large size, for which your tailor will make you a washing cover when you settle down, unless you take a case with you. A stick—you may get lame and require one—and a good stout riding whip. I always used a crop whip with a stout handle. If you have fur take it, but have a tin case on purpose for it—and for it only—and when not wearing it look at it frequently. The weather is often quite cold enough for fur. You will want also a couple of warm shawls and a railway rug. Two smaller wool shawls, for wrapping round the throat at night when out driving —that is, if you are at all delicate. Tin boxes of extra ribbons, bands, gloves, lace, and similar odds and ends.

A tin box, filled with needles, pins, threads, cottons, tapes, hooks and eyes, elastic, buttons, and all the thousand and one things wanted for mending and ordinary work. If you indulge in fancy work, paint, etch, &c., take out all things necessary for carrying on such amusements. Plenty of writing paper, envelopes—the tough sort of foreign paper is best—and some neat paper for invitations, &c. Extra brushes of all kinds, combs, soaps, and toilet necessaries you will also find useful, for bear in mind, that, though you can get all these things in India—in the larger stations at Parsee shops, or from the *cupra-wallahs* and *box-wallahs* who travel about from bungalow to bungalow—you will certainly be charged more than double the usual price, and get very inferior articles even then. Thread, for example, which, though it may bear the name of an English maker, is rotten and worthless; needles which snap off directly you use them, or have their eyes damaged; and pins from which the heads take the earliest opportunity of coming off. Such trifles take but little room in your boxes, and are of the greatest service. A sewing machine will also be of use, and if you have a hand one, I should advise your taking it, with extra needles, &c.

The Indian *durzee* is a very clever worker, good at imitating, but bad at originating. Give him a good pattern—you can get new ones by post from home as often as necessary—and he will turn out a dress very nicely, with strong, neat workmanship. He is a trifle slow, perhaps, but the work is good, not the red-hot needle, burning thread sort of work our dressmakers at home too often treat us to when they make up a dress in a hurry. My tailor was a very handsome young native, who rejoiced in the name of Iman Bux, and he remained with us all the time we were in India. A tailor is just as much your servant as your cook; you pay him so much a month; he feeds himself, as all native servants do, arrives about nine o'clock, and sits patiently working in your verandah till about six o'clock, or later if necessary, only appearing every now and again in the drawing-room, with the profoundest of salaams, to ask for more thread, or needles, or buttons, or tape. It is my private belief he kept a broken needle on purpose to show me, and got as many fresh ones as he could, considering them as a perquisite, as cooks do dripping in England. Certainly he had a wonderful faculty for breaking good English needles, but I heard my neighbours making just the same complaint of their *durzees*, so I suppose it is a trick peculiar to the class.

I have hitherto made no mention of boots and shoes. You must, however, start with a fair supply, and be sure you have an easy fit, as your feet swell in India in the hot weather. A tight boot is at any time an abomination—in India it entails downright misery. If you are sensible you will take neat buttoned boots for outdoor wear, with moderately high heels, not those fashionable, very small, high, brass-tipped affairs you now see ladies hobbling along upon, suffering pain and discomfort, consoled by the idea "that everybody wears them and they look so nice, you know." Do they? I like to see girls *walking*, not crawling with the aid of sticks or umbrellas, with the heels of their boots in the middle of their soles instead of in the proper place. That sort of thing does not answer for India, where, above all things, taking the trying climate into consideration, you need to study comfort. For this reason I advise boots for out-of-doors wear instead of shoes, as in the former you will not get your feet bitten with sandflies, ants, mosquitoes, and so forth.

Six pairs of boots, four thin and two thick, one pair of riding boots (long), six pairs of house shoes, four pairs of best evening shoes, and two pairs of a commoner kind ought to suffice for at least two or three years. Take extra bows, buckles, and buttons. Keep those you do not use in tin boxes, having the contents written outside on paper pasted on the lids. This I found a good plan, and should advise its being generally adopted for all tin boxes, as then you need only open the one you want, leaving the others securely soldered down.

For instance, two pairs of walking boots, one pair of tennis shoes (if you play tennis), one pair of house shoes, and two pairs of evening shoes are quite enough to have in use at one time. Even these must stand on a tin box or be kept in one—which is even better—the box itself being propped up on bricks to raise it from the floor, or the white ants will assuredly find it out. Shake any boot or shoe before putting it on, that is, if it has been standing out, as scorpions, centipedes, and similar small pests often make snug hiding places for themselves in such retreats.

CHAPTER III.

OUTFIT FOR THE MARRIED.

Table and Bed Linen—Coverings—Hangings—Miscellaneous Stores—General Household Requisites.

A MARRIED couple should certainly take with them house and table linen. It can, of course, be bought in India in the large stations, but is generally dressed for the market if of English or country manufacture, and is, moreover, of coarse quality and very expensive, more particularly the table linen (damask). It may look all right, be glossy and apparently fine; but the first wash will show how much you have been tricked. Calico is nearly always subjected to a surface gloss with what the natives call *conjee*, which is made with rice flour mixed in rice water and boiled, this preparation imparting a deceptive gloss to the material, and causing its texture to appear much finer than it really is. English goods are falsified, too, in much the same way, and for this reason their good name has declined in India. In the former case, when *conjee* has been used, the best test is to rub the material hard between the hands, in the same way as you would rub clothes in washing; the result, if the material is much sized, will be a very fine white powder. My advice, therefore, is to buy at home all you require in this department. Materials are not doctored up so much for the home market as for the export trade. This remark, though, perhaps, some may think severe, is, however, true.

In setting up an establishment in India you would not require nearly so much house linen as if commencing housekeeping at home; and, for this reason—your servants, though their name is legion, are not boarded or lodged at your expense. Moreover, if you have children, unless they are grown up, you will probably leave them at home; and you will be spared from furnishing so many. In this department, therefore, you need only reckon on your own requirements and on those of occasional guests.

Do not buy linen sheeting for Indian use.—People in India who value their health, never sleep in linen or wear linen underclothing, because it is apt to give a sudden chill to the body by checking its natural moisture, and is therefore dangerous. The following is a useful list:

> Six pairs of good strong calico sheets (full-sized).
> Four pairs of smaller size for single beds.
> Eighteen pillow slips.
> Two large counterpanes (white).
> Four small counterpanes (white).
> Two Austrian blankets (full size).
> Four ordinary blankets.
> Two horse rugs.

If four out of the eight warm coverings be striped, they may be used as wraps when travelling, as they will be more presentable in appearance than the ordinary blanket.

It may be thought that I have limited the blankets too much, but there are issued to the troops in India a most useful sort of light mattrass, which can be used either to lie on or as a covering. It is called a *ressaie*, and can be procured cheaply in almost any station, or even where there are no troops. It will last for years; we have two in our house at the present time, relics of our Indian sojourn, which are as good now as when they were bought, and are in daily use. You can, therefore, supplement the warmer portion of your bed furniture with *ressaies*, and I am sure you will never regret their purchase.

You will require further at least

> Two dozen bath towels,
> Two dozen fine towels,
> Four dozen commoner towels,

besides those you will want for board-ship use and for travelling.

A valise is always useful. With this you have materials at hand for your bed wherever you may have to sleep—at a dâk bungalow *en route*, or in rest-camps or huts; and at a few moments' notice you can make yourself fairly comfortable. In our valise, we carried one large mattrass, bolster, pillows, two of the inevitable *ressaies*, and the horse rugs, sheets and pillow cases, which, albeit rather cumbersome on many occasions, we found a great advantage.

Outfit for the Married.

With regard to table linen, the following list will be found quite sufficient for some years, and when it requires replenishing a box from England will set you going again :

You will require at least :

> Six ordinary dinner cloths.
> Six larger, and of better quality.
> Four very large and very fine, for dinner parties, with slips of same quality damask.
> Six breakfast cloths.
> Six luncheon cloths.
> Twelve tray cloths (small).
> Twelve sideboard cloths.
> Two dozen table napkins, matching ordinary dinner cloths.
> Two dozen, matching, better quality.
> Two dozen matching best dinner cloths.
> Two dozen matching breakfast cloths.
> Two dozen matching luncheon cloths.
> Four dozen common, for fish, &c.

Table napkins are used at every meal in India, and you require a good stock, as the rough treatment they get from the dhobie wears them out very quickly. By having them to match the various table cloths, however, you economise a good deal.

Tea cloths, glass cloths, kitchen cloths, and dusters should be taken out in the piece, and made up by your durzee when you reach your destination.

The frequency with which the natives lose or make away with the dusters you give them for use in their various departments is astonishing. Everyone complains how rapidly the *jhárans*, as your servants call them, disappear. Your *khánsámán* (cook) must have them supplied to him, your *khitmutgár* (table attendant), bearer (butler), *syce* (groom), *mehter* (sweeper), and your *ayah* (maid) have also to be furnished; and my firm belief is that one and all keep a very old torn and dilapidated *jháran* by them to show you when you exclaim that "they cannot possibly want new dusters again when you so very lately provided them"; but the unanswerable argument is, "If we have not good dusters, how can we do our work as the Mem-Sahib likes us to?" and the unfortunate Mem-Sahib gives in, and distributes new dusters all round. The only check on this inordinate love of dusters is to get them brought on the weekly day when the clothes are counted over in your presence by the *dhobie;* each servant bringing his own dusters and counting them before you. It is a tiresome business, but

I found on adopting it that it answered fairly well. For though a few dusters, tea cloths, glass cloths, &c., occasionally may not be a serious loss, still when it goes on repeatedly, a stop must be put to it. I am sure that the battle of the jhárans might well be chronicled. At home you can buy material for these necessary articles cheaply enough, and at the stores, or at some wholesale house, a large quantity will not reach a serious sum. The stuff you will get in India for the purpose is comparatively worthless, washing to pieces directly.

If you have a fancy for making your bedrooms pretty, and like etched or crewel-worked mats, towels artistically bordered with impossible flowers, and teapots, saucers, and the like on your five o'clock tea cloths—which, by the way, I had forgotten to mention before — by all means indulge your taste; they make your rooms look pretty and well cared for, though many people contemptuously call them dust traps and nests for insects. I am bound to say they are the latter, and for that reason I preferred my toilet table in its pristine beauty, unadorned by mats or muslin draperies.

But there are other purchases for your house besides the ordinary table and house linen which I should strongly advise you to make before you leave England, such as chintz or cretonne for your drawing-room curtains, sofa and chair coverings. You can now get such pretty patterns in cretonnes, and so very reasonably, that there can be no difficulty in suiting yourself. Take out in the piece enough of one sort for all the coverings and hangings, with the necessary lining, cords, ribbons, braid, &c., to make them up nicely, not forgetting stout cotton for working with. I would also suggest that you take muslin for window blinds, *écru* lace curtains, several pairs alike. The windows in most Indian houses are very high, and you will very likely have to join your curtains, which, if they are of the same pattern, can easily be managed. A piece of crash, either velvet (cotton backed) or cloth, should be added with a view to ornamental antimacassar making for mantel-piece boards, brackets, picture frames, &c.; together with plenty of that cheap, coarse, but effective-looking furniture lace, which can now be bought nearly everywhere, and makes very ornamental fringes for the mantel-piece board, small five o'clock tea tables, wall glasses, brackets, and the like. It is astonishing how easily, with the aid of such trifles and some cleverness with the fingers, you can make a bare room look fairly pretty —at all events, endurable. I shall have more to say later on about Indian rooms; I may mention, however, that you will require some fancy nails for your amateur ornamental carpentering, and same neat braid for headings.

Some husband will exclaim "What a quantity of room these things will take! You will require a ship to yourself at least!"

I do not suggest for an instant that you should consider these extras as personal luggage, knowing very well the difficulty attendant on too great a number of boxes to be taken with you. One very large wooden tin-lined box ought, with careful packing, to hold all these things, which I will term household goods; and with the glass and crockery in another box or barrel, it can be sent on before you, *viâ* Suez Canal, to meet you on arrival at your landing port, when you can either have it sent on direct by luggage train, if you are going anywhere on the line of rail, or else take it with you. In my own case we pursued the plan I here recommend, sending on our heavy luggage before. Of course we insured it, which I may add, is a very necessary precaution.

Money spent in such purchases as I have just described is in no danger of being wasted, as people who do not know India might possibly imagine. Good house and table linen always command a sale there, if offered, and the same may be said of any little fancy articles you may not want, when you either go home or leave one station for another.

CHAPTER IV.

OUTFIT FOR GENTLEMEN.

General Remarks—Clothing—Dress and Morning Suits—Underclothing—Boots and Shoes—Toilet Requisites—Shooting and Fishing Equipment—Saddlery—Stationery—Plate.

A GENTLEMAN going out to India in these days does not require so large an outfit as in years gone by, and for various reasons I would strongly advise moderation as regards outfit to be taken. It is certainly a mistake to take out a great number of cloth suits, and it is better to have new suits forwarded occasionally from a London tailor than to start with too many. The charges of the Calcutta and Bombay tailors moreover are excessive, and none but the extravagant would dream of replenishing wardrobes at their hands when it is easy to order things from home.

It is an advantage to gentlemen that the fashion of their garments does not change so often as in the case of ladies' dresses. Hence an evening suit will last for years if properly cut at the outset, and the same remark applies to a frock coat and to morning suits.

Again so much white clothing is worn in India that cloth suits are rather at a discount, especially in the hot weather. White uniform coats, and white morning and lounging coats are seen on all sides, except, of course, on dress occasions; and they are economical to wear in a country where washing is not expensive.

Though in cold weather cloth coats, of course, come to the fore, white clothing and the old familiar sun hat, *solar topee*, is the usual attire in the hot season. The native tailors (*durzees*) make up these white suits admirably, provided they have a good pattern to cut by, which can easily be provided by bringing out a well cut suit from home. American drill can be bought very cheaply in most stations in India, as it is largely purchased by the troops, and so can *khakee*, a light drab stuff, which wears and washes well; also light native cloths, such as camels' hair, *puttoo*, &c., which are cheap, and make up well for loose lounging suits.

Flannel shirts and suits for tennis, racquets, cricket, and so forth, should, however, be brought out, as it is difficult to purchase good flannel in the country; but all linen and cotton articles, and material for sleeping suits, can be bought in India at fairly reasonable prices. The following list will, I think, be found ample to start with :—

> Three dozen good longcloth shirts, linen fronted, with linen wristbands.
> Six dozen shirt collars.
> Three dozen extra wristbands (if worn).
> One dozen flannel shirts.
> One dozen vests.
> One dozen pairs of drawers (merino).
> One sleeping suit (thin).
> Four ditto, thicker material, flannel.

The thin sleeping suit is to be taken as a pattern, the number to be made up to six on arrival in India, extra material being either taken out or purchased there.

> Four dozen pairs of cotton socks, unbleached.
> Two dozen pairs warmer for cold weather.
> One dozen silk (spun) socks for evening wear.
> Four dozen cambric pocket handkerchiefs, plain, or with coloured borders, as preferred.
> Two dozen silk ditto.
> Four dozen white ties.
> One dozen coloured washing ditto.
> Four pairs of braces.
> One dressing gown, flannel.
> One dressing gown of native cloth, to be made in India, from pattern of flannel one, for cold weather.
> One white morning suit (American drill), to be taken out as a pattern for others to be made from; four at least will be required, or perhaps six.
> One loose morning coat (white), as pattern for three additional.
> Twelve white waistcoats.
> Three dozen white towels.
> Two dozen bath towels.

If the gentleman be single, and takes out no house linen, he must add to his outfit—

> Four pairs of sheets. One mattrass.
> Eight pillow cases. Two pillows.
> Two blankets. A valise to pack them in.

He should also purchase on arrival at his station

> Two ressaies.
> Eight tablecloths of good damask.
> Two dozen table napkins.
> One clothes bag, with a good lock to it, for use on the voyage.

The table and house linen will not, of course, be required until the final destination is reached.

Respecting cloth clothing, it is difficult to state any precise number of suits, for much depends on vocation, whether officer or civilian. Anyhow he will want—

> One good black dress suit for evening wear.
> One extra pair dress trousers.
> One frock coat.
> One waterproof coat.
> One thin dust overcoat.
> One medium thickness.
> One warm overcoat for cold weather.
> Two ordinary everyday suits, not too thick.
> Two strong shooting suits (if he shoots).
> One warm suit for cold weather wear.
> One tall hat for dress occasions.
> Two deerstalkers.
> Two soft wideawakes.
> One *solar topee*, to be bought on arrival.

With respect to officers, I have not mentioned uniform, the requirements depending much on personal predilection and much on the customs of different regiments.

A good stock of boots and shoes will, of course, be necessary, say:

> Two pairs thick shooting boots.
> One pair fishing boots (high).
> One pair riding boots (high).
> Four pairs ordinary walking boots or shoes.
> Two pairs tennis shoes.
> Two pairs dress shoes.
> Two pairs slippers.

Ample provision of gloves should also be taken—for riding and driving, dogskin; for ordinary and evening wear, kid. These should be kept in tin cases. To these are to be added ordinary white ties, and black silk ties for evening dress, and coloured silk scarves or ties for morning wear.

Various extras are necessary, in the shape of sponges, sponge-bags, brushes for hair, teeth, nails, hats, and clothes; a box of

Pears' soap, unquestionably the best and hardest for taking abroad; a medicine case fitted with such medicines as quinine, chlorodyne, aperient pills, Eno's fruit salt, mustard leaves, Jamaica ginger (Oxley's essence), and any other medicines which may be occasionally wanted.

A tin dressing case, fitted with the usual requisites, razors, strops, and so forth.

A tin dispatch box—the "A B C" is the most useful.

Plenty of stationery, including tough foreign paper and envelopes, foolscap and official envelopes to match, common note paper for *chits*, better paper for answering invitations, visiting-cards, pens, sealing wax, pencils, indiarubber, and the like, which in India are all expensive and inferior in quality. Sketch books and colour box will suggest themselves to the artistically inclined.

A good gun, a rifle, a revolver, some fishing tackle, a telescope, a pair of opera glasses, a deck chair, table lamp, one of the latest maps of India, a few useful books, and a case of saddlery, are so many luxuries which can, of course, be omitted where economy dictates; but in India they are capable of adding much to the comfort of life, whether civil or military.

Saddlery, it may be remarked is now a less necessary part of the outfit than formerly. Very fair saddles can be easily and reasonably bought in India secondhand. Certainly they are less difficult to obtain than in days gone by, when taking them out was regarded as a good investment. Still, an English made saddle, bearing the stamp of a good maker, is rarely an article to hang on hand if you wish to part with it.

Sport in India is obtainable everywhere; and to a sportsman a gun is indispensable. It may be bought by chance out there, but it would be better to buy one of a good maker in England. The sportsman, indeed, may revel to his heart's content, and choose at will from snipe to black buck. Big game is not so easily found now as formerly, and considerable expense is incurred in seeking it; but for anyone who possesses a good gun, a rifle, a nag, and a couple or so of dogs, an hour or two's shooting in the morning, or a day's sport, is nearly always to be had in the vicinity of small stations, the best shooting being, of course, in the less frequented districts.

With regard to the packing of the outfit, the same sort of baggage is required for both ladies and gentlemen, and on this subject I shall have some suggestions to make in a future chapter. I may mention here that, besides the ordinary trunks of regulation size, a leather bag, for cabin use, square-mouthed, with a good lock, should be provided; some tin regimental cases for uniform, a tin box for extra brushes, a tin case for medicine box, and another for dressing case, or else the dressing case itself should be of tin. Avoid leather cases as much as possible in favour of tin. The white ants revel in leather, and, moreover, articles kept in it will become mildewed.

A small box fitted with plated spoons and forks will be found useful, containing, say, four large and four small forks, four large, four dessert, four teaspoons and two salt spoons; six large knives, and six small ditto; two pairs of carvers, and a tiny cruet stand. If these things are fitted into a baize-lined wooden box, then an extra tin case will be required. Ordinary nickel-plated articles are the best kind to take out, certainly not silver, as they would be stolen by the natives very soon; and good nickel-plated articles look very presentable, take a good polish, and wear very well. I speak from experience. Those I bought ten years ago look now as well as ever; constant use in India has not deteriorated them, and the plating, being on a white metal, shows no sign of rubbing off.

CHAPTER V.

THE VOYAGE OUT.

Requisites on Board Ship—Sea-Sickness—Amusements.

HAVING properly packed and duly forwarded to the place of embarkation your heavy luggage which is destined for the "baggage room,"—supposing that you intend to proceed the whole way by sea, and having also packed a change of clothing, to be worn in the Red Sea, in a box marked to that effect, your next consideration is what you will actually need in respect of dress, wraps, and the like on the voyage.

Do not encumber yourself with over much linen or too many dresses, but allow enough for the time, reckoning it at a month; it will probably be rather less, but then, after landing, you will most likely have a railway journey of a few days, before reaching your final destination, or, again, you may rest a few days, either at Bombay or wherever you have to land. Whether you make your voyage in a troop-ship, in a P. and O. steamer, or in a steamer of any other line, your requirements will be much the same.

The usual season for sailing on a voyage to India is in the late autumnal and winter months—October, November, December, or January—because thereby your arrival happens in the cold weather, and you have time fairly to settle down before the hot season sets in. And, besides, you have not to undergo a railway journey in the heat, which to those fresh out from England, is very trying, and sometimes fatal. January is, perhaps, the best month for landing; the climate is then very pleasant—hot in the middle of the day, but cool, not to say cold, in the mornings and evenings.

Take your oldest linen for the occasion. Washing cannot be done on board, and you must, therefore, have sufficient for at least a month. This quantity will take up a good deal of space, but that drawback cannot be helped. You can pack some in the box containing the change of clothing for Suez, or in your second trunk, placed in the "Present Use Baggage Room." Two trunks of regulation size No. 3 you are allowed to have with you in your cabin; but in a troop-ship—supposing you are going by one—you will find it more convenient to keep one of these, as well as your clothes bag, with lock and key, in the "Present Use Baggage Room" where you can have access to it every day, rather than have two boxes in the limited space you will have at your disposal, and in the place of a second trunk, to employ the square-mouthed hand-bag I have mentioned. This will hold the odds and ends in everyday use, and avoid having to drag your trunk from under your berth for everything you want during the day. Your single trunk you will then pack with a portion of your linen, a pair of thick boots, a pair of thickish shoes with not too thin soles, as the decks are often damp from frequent washing, and a pair of lighter shoes for evening wear. These, with the boots or shoes you will be wearing when you go on board, you will find enough; but do not let them be too tight fitting or made with very high heels, or you will be sorry for yourself; let them be easy and comfortable, not new, but such as you have had in use.

It is not at all necessary to appear frequently in different dresses; for travelling you may wear the same dress (which should be of a sensible kind) either cloth or strong serge, made *trotteuse*, with extra jacket and hat of same materials, every morning; you will probably change it for dinner in favour of an old black silk or cashmere and silk, a demi-toilette dress which has already seen service; this can always be made pretty, for evening wear, by adding lace round the neck and sleeves, and coloured ribbon bows, matching those in your cap, if you wear caps. A dress of this sort is in better taste for the purpose than a more elaborate toilette; though I have seen ladies, brides especially, appear in fresh costumes nearly every day; this looks absurd; for though they had many dresses, they might resist the temptation to wear them when on board ship.

This old evening dress—you see I only allow one—must be packed in your box, and also an extra one for morning wear, of some warm material, in case you injure the one you are wearing, and have to make a change. You will require a shady hat for deck wear, as even before you reach the Red Sea you may find the want of it. A flannel dressing gown and a short flannel jacket for night wear should be taken also, as at first you will find the nights very cold. Some favourite books should have a place in the bottom of your trunk, with your working and writing materials, and, if you are artistic, your drawing materials also. Take a tin box for holding the gloves you have in use, which should be either dogskin or *gants de Suède* for every day wear, and black kid for better occasions; you may not use these, but still you should put them in; and this tin box will also hold extra ribbons. Another box (cardboard) for collars and cuffs, which for the voyage should be paper ones, besides a handkerchief box, a warm red woollen shawl for evening wear (not white, it would soil so soon), a sunshade, and some towels, bath and ordinary, for these are not provided. You can sometimes get towels washed on board by one of the soldiers' wives, as I did mine, but you had better take enough for the whole time. Your one trunk will by this time be full, and your hand bag will come into use for the rest of your cabin necessaries.

Do not forget toilet requisites—brushes and combs in a bag, mirror, sponge also in a bag, nail brush and tooth brush in division of sponge bag, nightgown case, with nightgown, &c. This you should have large enough to hold the flannel jacket also, as in that case you can in the morning fold up night things and jacket, and deposit them in the case on your berth. Take some cakes of Pears' Soap, a good sized bottle of Eau de Cologne, a bottle of essence of Jamaica ginger, which is good for sea sickness, a few drops on white lump sugar taken every morning being very beneficial, and even if you do not suffer from that distressing malady, you will find the ginger act as an excellent stomachic. Provide yourself also with bottles of sal volatile, toilet vinegar, Eno's Fruit Salt, chlorodyne, quinine, mustard leaves, pills, smelling salts, a case of sticking plaister, and a small bottle of brandy or whisky. You can, of course, get spirits on board, but you may want same in case of sudden illness in the night, when it would be impossible to procure it. Have a glass or silver drinking cup, one or two wax candles, night lights, a taper case, with glass protector, matches, and tapers to fit it. You are not allowed to use lights in cabins other than those provided, but you will want your tapers and lights on your railway journey. You should certainly have a work case in your bag, well filled with all necessaries for mending, plenty of pins, needles, and hair-pins, a good knife, a pair of scissors, button hook, pencil in a leather case, and an extra hand glass. If one side of your bag is fitted as a dressing bag, you will find it the more useful. A small tin containing white lump sugar, and small packets of cocoa, with another of biscuits, should also find a place. These you can replenish when necessary from your other trunk in the "Present Use Baggage Room." A fan, a note-book, and any other small books, such as your Prayer-book, in a case, may also be put in, with a guide book, a small Hindustani manual and dictionary, for you should certainly, whether lady or gentleman (I am writing more particularly for ladies now), endeavour to learn something of the language while going out. You are sure to find some one to help you in doing so, and even a little knowledge you will find of great assistance when you land. Besides your trunk and your hand-bag you must have a bundle of wraps, an ulster, waterproof cloak to wrap round you, railway rug, and extra warm shawls. These can all be strapped with your umbrella on to your deck chair. I had forgotten to mention the chair, but you should certainly take one, for you will find it a great comfort. This arrangement will make but one package of the whole, only your wraps must have extra straps also (those with a handle are the most convenient). You will find your extra wraps very useful on deck, more especially in the early part of the voyage, for if the weather be fine, you should be as much on deck as possible, and you will be less likely to suffer from sea-sickness than if you remained in the stuffy little cabins below.

In the "Ladies' Cabin" there are generally about seven berths, sometimes more if the ship is crowded—I am writing now of troop-ships. In the Nursery from fourteen to twenty berths are arranged, and in other cabins three, four, or five, according to the size and the number of ladies on board.

Various regulations are prescribed respecting meals, lights in cabins, wet clothes, soiled linen, and similar matters, which are generally posted up in the saloon; and a study of these should be made as early as possible after getting on board. The captain generally goes round the cabins twice a week, to see that all is in order, and that the rules are complied with.

Baths are easily to be obtained, either hot or cold; but the early morning bath in fresh sea water each day is, to my mind, one of the charms of a sea voyage—only you need to sponge yourself with other water afterwards.

A few words about sea-sickness. I hold Jamaica ginger, as I have before observed, to be an excellent remedy; but some cases are so obstinate as to yield to none of the ordinary recipes; and in that event a doctor should be consulted. The morning bath, keeping as much on deck as possible, constantly nibbling a hard dry biscuit, avoiding tea, coffee, and sloppy foods generally, placing, in violent attacks, a mustard-leaf on the pit of the stomach and a bit of ice in the mouth, are all worth trying; and remember always that the more you struggle and fight against sea-sickness the more likely you are to overcome it; while, on the contrary, giving way at first is likely to make you more or less a sufferer all the voyage. Many people, no doubt, are habitually sea-sick on even the shortest voyage and in the calmest weather; but I believe that very many who give in might, with more strength of mind, get over it.

To those who like the sea, the voyage is very pleasant; there are generally many nice people on board, and, if troops are carried, sometimes a band, and on fine nights dancing on deck, or singing, glee parties, and so on; very often amateur theatricals are got up, and come off the night before the port is reached. There is usually a library on board, and there is no reason why, with much that is new to interest and with pleasant society, the time should not pass quickly and agreeably.

I happened to go out before the opening of the Suez Canal, and therefore had to land at Alexandria, go by rail to Suez, and take the other ship there. Now, however, no change is necessary, unless, it may be, the overland route be preferred to the sea. The journey by rail across the desert was to me the most trying part of the whole trip—dusty, hot, and thoroughly uncomfortable we were. A more disagreeable day I never spent, or a more fatiguing one.

CHAPTER VI.

PLACES EN ROUTE.

Malta—Alexandria—the Khedive's Palace—Port Said—the Suez Canal—the Red Sea—Aden—Off the Port of Bombay—Approach—the Town—Objects and Places of Interest.

ON the voyage out the steamers generally stop at Gibraltar, Malta, Port Said, Suez, and Aden, before reaching Bombay; and the distances, from place to place, are:—Portsmouth to Gibraltar, 1127 miles; Malta, 988; Port Said, 937; Suez, 88; Perim, 1201 (no stoppage here); Aden, 97; Bombay, 1644.

At Gibraltar the P. and O. boats usually make a stoppage of about six hours; but the troop-ships very often do not stop at all, unless troops have to be landed or embarked, and in any case the time allowed is too short to do much more than stroll about a little, or hire a horse and see as much as you can in a short time.

At Malta more time is allowed, especially by troop-ship, and some of the chief spots of interest can be visited, as the ship remains about twenty-four hours. Carriages can be obtained at reasonable prices. The Governor's Palace—the former Palace of the Grand Masters—should certainly be visited, as its corridors, chambers, and the Knights' Armoury, are very interesting. The Church of St. John is very beautiful, the New Market is a fine building, while the coral, silver, and lace shops in the Strada Reale are very tempting. At the Theatre Royal, near the Porta Reale Gate, there is generally something worth hearing; it was burnt down in 1873, but is now, I believe, perfectly restored. In returning home from India, we went on shore at Malta, and slept there the night the ship remained in port, but very nearly paid dearly for doing so, as when we were about to return to the vessel our nurse and child could not be found, having strayed into the market, where eventually they were discovered. The time for sailing was nearly up, and we had to make our driver literally gallop his horse down a steep hill, and were obliged to row off in great hurry, only succeeding in reaching the vessel as she was beginning to move. It was indeed a narrow chance. Mem.: When on shore at Malta, especially with a nurse and baby, do not put off the return on board till the last moment. A word about the Maltese shopkeepers. They certainly have lovely things on offer—such coral, such lace, such silver filagree! But they have two prices, one for travellers and the other for residents—if possible, therefore, get a resident to make your purchases, if you happen to know any one in the island. Moreover, they do not bring out their best articles for ship folks, but try to impose inferior ones on those who cannot very readily detect the difference.

By the overland route you would stop at Alexandria, and make the journey to Suez by rail. At Alexandria there is a good deal to see. The P. and O. Hotel is one of the nicest to stay at, though Abbat's is, I believe, considered the best. We were very comfortable at the first-named, and it is pleasantly situated. The Khedive's Palace is one of the places to see; the building is not very ornamental outside, but some of the rooms are very handsome, of good size, with inlaid floors, highly polished, and some of ebony and ivory. The hangings, also, are of handsome silk and damask, and very good taste is displayed in general. Curiosity led me to turn up the cloth on the dining table. Its legs were of such beautiful mahogany that I fancied the top would be equally handsome; but it was of plain deal in the centre, with mahogany ends. One room was painted around in neutral tint with views of Rome, and had a marble floor and a handsome fountain in the centre. To get admission, an order must be obtained from the vakil (steward). You should also, if you have time, see Pompey's Pillar; and if you wish to see these sights, you had better select a dragoman at once, from among the yelling horde who surround you directly on landing, on the presumption that he will keep off the rest. A crowd of natives is by no means pleasant to be mixed with. They positively revel in dirt; each man, woman, and child you pass appears more and more dirty; and *bouquet d'Alexandre* has only to be smelt to be fully believed in. They resemble the Scriptural sow, and literally wallow in filth. At Suez they are even more miserably squalid, every other child appearing to be afflicted with ophthalmia. For this reason, one should be very careful never to allow flies to settle on the face, as they are credited with carrying the infection.

At Port Said the steamers stop only a short time, and the voyage through the canal is not very enlivening, particularly if you ground once or twice. Port Said is a town created entirely by the canal, and as the traffic yearly increases in importance so does the place flourish. It is dirty withal, and by no means agreeable or interesting to stop at. Beginning here, the canal passes a shallow lagune, which is called Menzaleh; its banks generally swarm with water fowl, flamingoes, and various other birds; the western lagune is called Ballah; then comes Lake Tismah, on the northern edge of which is Ismailia, a sort of half-way small town between Port Said and Suez. Then the canal crosses Lake Tismah to Toussoum, and thence to the Great and Little Bitter Lakes, next to which is the Suez lagune, and so into the Red Sea. Oh! that Red Sea! its very name is nauseating. In it one is sure to be hot, and if there is any breeze it is certain to be the wrong one. Awnings are put up, lighter articles of clothing come out, people become irritable, punkahs vibrate not half fast enough, nights are suffocatingly hot, and days are worse. The temperature is hot all the year round—80deg. to 90deg. in the cabins, even from October to March, and it is not at all wise to put off the passage beyond the latter month. If there is any wind it is a hot one, and the heat creates intense thirst. A dose or two of Eno's Fruit Salt should be taken in order to ward off fever. Soda water and lime juice, or soda water and milk, if you can get milk, are good drinks to take. Spirits and wine should be avoided, as they only heat the body instead of cooling it. Cold tea is refreshing, but should not be made too strong, and is not always easy to get. The tea and coffee on board ship are never very good, tea tasting like coffee, and coffee like tea, condensed milk, moreover, giving both a disagreeable flavour.

Aden is utterly uninteresting—a barren rocky shore without a vestige of green. The natives (Soumalis) are rough, wild-looking creatures, with shocks of red or yellow hair. They swim round the ship in shoals like fish, and dive with wonderful expertness, for small bits of money, bringing them up from a considerable depth.

The steamers usually coal here, thereby occupying some eight or ten hours. Meanwhile life is a burden; the decks are filthy, coal dust floats about in small particles, and penetrates nose, mouth, eyes, and hair. A good plan is to wear a gauze veil if you remain on board; but most people, uninviting as Aden looks, go on shore. Various articles of Indian and Chinese workmanship can be bought here; also coral and ostrich feathers—the natural undyed feathers. The large white and black ones they ask a long price for, but the greyish small feathers you can buy cheaply, and they are very useful, especially for children's hats. I have some now I bought coming home, which dye and re-dye, and seem never to wear out.

After leaving Aden the rest of the voyage to Bombay is performed in about seven days, and if the steamer arrives in Bombay Harbour during the daytime the sight is very pretty—Malabar Hill on one side, and Colaba, where the lighthouse is situated, on the other, and the town, with its large and, many of them, finely built, handsome houses. Steeples of churches are to be seen rising above the other buildings. On either side of the bay mountains mark the western boundaries of the Indian continent. The Island of Bombay lies to the left, fronted by a fortress mounted with guns. At this time of the year—I suppose the traveller to have landed in December or January—Bombay looks green and pretty; there is no lack of foliage, groves of date and other palms are dotted about, and the country houses which lie on the Malabar Hill side are almost hidden with fine trees.

When the steamer is sighted by the Colaba lookout, who is stationed by the flagstaff at the top of the lighthouse, she is immediately signalled. If she is a mail steamer, a gun is fired and the mail signal run up, and then her arrival is telegraphed all over India. On reaching her anchorage, her mails are first landed, and then her passengers go on shore. If she is a troopship, she is first visited by the resident transport officer. These vessels generally anchor opposite the Apollo Bunder, and the P. and O. steamers higher up the harbour, at Mazagon. If troops have to be landed, this is rarely done at once; probably the debarkation will take place early the next morning, and the soldiers will be taken straight from the ship to the nearest railway station. I remember well the misery of turning out, almost before it was light, on a cold, raw morning, going in a steam launch to the station, and waiting there at least two hours until all had arrived and the train was ready to start. Anyhow, there will be some hours to spend in Bombay; and if you are travelling on your own account and able to take time, the hours

D

will probably lengthen into days, as there is much to see. There are good hotels; Watson's is the nearest to the Apollo Bunder; Pallinjee's, at Byculla, nearest to the station; at either you may be very comfortable, but at both you will find the charges pretty high. Some of the buildings are very fine—the National Bank, English and Native Mercantile Offices, the Municipal Offices, Secretarial Library, Post Office, High Court, &c. Of clubs there are the Bombay Club, Byculla Club, Cricket, Yacht, and others. The cathedral is well worth a visit; the Victoria Gardens also, if you care to see various specimens of exotics and natural flora; it was originally established by Dr. Birdwood, whose name is now famous in connection with Indian industrial art. The lighthouse on Colaba Hill is within a short drive, and the view from it lovely; there is also an observatory at Colaba. The Vehar Waterworks and Lake (Salsette Hills) are also within a drive, but rather a long one. The Elephanta Caves on the Gharapuri Island you certainly must see, if you stay in Bombay long enough. They are one of the chief sights in the neighbourhood, and a trip to them, either by steamer or sailing boat across the harbour, is very delightful, and with a favourable breeze takes no more than two hours. One of the roomy, short-masted fishing boats, lateen rigged, with dark brown sails, is a very comfortable craft for an expedition of the sort. Gharapuri, as the natives call the island, is about five miles from Bombay mainland, lying to the east; and, as the island is clothed with verdure down to the water's edge, and the trees are chiefly palms of various sorts, it presents, as you approach it, a very pretty appearance. From the top—for there is a steep ascent from the landing place to the caves—there is a lovely view. In the extreme distance are the far-famed Ghauts, looking very hazy in the glare of the sunlight; then the dark narrow neck of land, Colaba Point, with the lighthouse at its extremity, from which an expanse of rippling water reaches to the feet, the Islands of Salsette and Bombay, and Butcher's Island, breaking it up. Along the line of shore from Colaba we trace various points to the Apollo Bunder, a very favourite resort in the cool of the evening for the Europeans in Bombay. Then Bombay itself, with its numerous buildings; and between us and the town is a perfect forest of masts, the shipping of all nations. The caves are too well known to need a special description, but they are undoubtedly worth a visit before you pursue your journey up country, and for this reason I have mentioned them.

CHAPTER VII.

TRAVELLING UP COUNTRY.

Railway Travelling—Refreshments—Provision for the Journey—Scenery—Jubbulpore—The " Marble Rocks "—Allahabad—Confluence of the Jumna and the Ganges—Cawnpore—The Cholera—The Memorable Well—Hotels—Charges—Agra—The Taj—An Indian Sunset—Night Travelling—Scenery—Mooltan.

RAILWAY travelling in India is never very agreeable, the dust and glare being very trying to the eyes, and the rate of progression slow. I will suppose that you have a long distance to go before you reach your destination. Say you are going to Lahore. You will have 1558 miles of rail to travel, and, by passenger train, will take about five days and nights doing the distance. If time is no great object and you are not travelling with troops, I should advise this journey being broken at Jubbulpore, Allahabad, Cawnpore, and Toondla, for Agra. If you are going further than Lahore, say, to Mooltan, then another stoppage might be made at Lahore. By resting in this way, and travelling as much as possible by night, you will not feel the journey so fatiguing, and you will, besides, have an opportunity of seeing some of the chief places of interest *en route*.

For troops the first resting place is Deolalee, about 113 miles from Bombay, this being the "rest camp" up and down, where accommodation is provided in huts, and there is a mess for bachelor officers.

The scenery on the line up from Bombay to Egatpoora, at the foot of the Western Ghauts, is in places very lovely and varied; the colour of the distant Ghauts, which are very singular and striking, is mostly red, deepening to purple in the shadows.

For about thirty or forty miles from Bombay the country is level, and at intervals there are pretty glimpses of the sea, into which flows the Tanna river, the line running at times quite close to its banks, and across it in one place over a well-built viaduct. The Callian river is also close to the line, and, as the country is well wooded, the effects here and there of water, tree, rock, and sky—which is in India rarely obscured by clouds—are most picturesque. Then the line commences to rise rapidly, and the scenery becomes more rugged and grand; the high red peaks of the nearer hills alternate with the deep wooded ravines, presenting every shade of green and yellow, while always in the distance is the line of Ghauts with their varied shading. The line turns about a great deal during the ascent, and the engines (there are usually two for the steepest parts) are in one place shifted to the rear of the train, and the ascent forwards is continued in that way. The incline is very considerable, 1ft. in 30ft., and the Poonah Ghauts are even steeper. When Egatpoora is passed the hills decrease in size, and the country becomes less interesting. If the journey from Bombay to Jubbulpore is made without a break—that is, beyond the occasional half hours allowed for refreshment—it takes twenty-seven and a half hours, and travellers should provide themselves with refreshment, and not trust to procuring it on the journey, for sufficient time is not allowed to obtain a comfortable meal; the viands are untempting, indigestible, greasy, and always the same "muttony chop," "mourghee" (fowl), and beefsteaks, much resembling india-rubber. We always took provisions with us on every railway journey—hard-boiled eggs, cold teal, cold chicken, salt, mustard, and pepper, bread, fruit, ice, cold tea, soda water, claret, brandy, and filtered water in a jar or in bottles. These things were all packed in a "tiffin basket," with iron plates and cups enamelled inside. It is a great mistake to drink much when travelling, but soda water and pure water should always be provided, brandy in case of illness, together with claret; do not trust to getting water at the stations you pass. In India, moreover, never drink water that has not been boiled and filtered; certainly it should have undergone the latter process. A pocket filter should be part of everybody's kit, man or woman, but I much fear this is the first time I have mentioned it. Readers, however, should do as Captain Cuttle did, "make a note of it," and forgive the omission; it is an indispensable requisite. Cold tea is an excellent drink in India, especially in the hot weather, when it should be iced; yet it must not be made too strong. It is as refreshing a beverage as can be found, and I have known men who drank it during a hard day's shooting in preference to anything else.

The railway carriages are fairly comfortable, and one is rarely crowded; the seats turn up to form beds. There is ample space underneath the seats for such luggage as is necessary to have in the carriage with you—such as wraps, tiffin baskets, and hand bags. The windows are in many cases made of blue tinted glass, and have jalousies to shelter you from the sun; the roofs are double, with projecting eaves, and the lamps give a fair light. Each carriage, also, has a retiring room, conveniently furnished with washing stand, water laid on, looking glass, &c. If you travel by night, which should be done as much as possible, some hours' sleep can generally be procured, at least by those who can sleep in a train. I, for one, cannot, and the night journeys in consequence always fatigued me; the nights seemed terribly long, and I felt glad when day broke, for the tedium was then over, and the light gradually appearing re-awakened interest, in that it revealed the dim country round, which became each moment more distinct, showed the tops of trees and the parklike fields, while here and there one caught glimpses of animal life, startled deer, jackals stealing away from the fields, huge birds, and the like; and as the train passed villages the natives were seen, in their white robes, or else clothed merely in the primitive *dhotee*, going out to their early labour, driving their cattle before them and taking them to drink.

Indian railway stations are generally pretty; little gardens gay with flowers are cultivated around, pots of flowering plants are dotted about, and beautiful creepers twine over the verandahs and roofs of the buildings. The nights, be it remembered, are cold, and you are glad of all the wraps you have brought. Here I would suggest always to have ends of wax candles or else tapers in your bag, with a good supply of matches, for the lamps may go out, as I remember they did one night when we were travelling, and it is not pleasant to be in the dark, especially if the carriage is not filled by your own party. Soap, too, you should have with you, and towels. Various medicines, such as I before advised, should find a place in your bag. Essence of beef tea might also be given room with advantage. A flannel hood, to slip on over the head at night, when lying down and the hat is removed, is a great comfort, and prevents danger from draught and the fear of neuralgia or stiff neck.

Soon after the sun rises the carriages become hot, and in the colder weather, and by noon, even in February, will be almost unbearable; but as the sum sinks lower they grow cool again.

At Jubbulpore Jackson's Family Hotel is fairly good, and has the advantage, if you are travelling with troops, of being near the "rest camp." The comfort of sleeping in bed, with a good wash, and a meal taken at leisure is always appreciated after travelling.

Jubbulpore is rather prettily situated under a rocky height; it boasts of three hotels. The one I have mentioned had quite a baronial appearance—a large white structure, with verandahs and ornamental columns. The deep verandahs built all round the Indian houses make them look very much larger than they really are. The town boasts a church, a high school, a branch bank, a Government school of industry, a prison, a museum, a library; various factories for jute, lac dye, and, I believe, opium, and the cantonments are of good size. If you remain a whole day, an excursion would naturally be made to the far-famed "marble rocks." They can be reached in two miles by rail from Mirganj station, and are within a drive of twelve miles from the town. A dâk bungalow will be found at the rocks, from which there is a fine view of them; but take your "tiffin" with you as usual, for though the bungalow boasts a *khánsámán* (cook), his resources are limited. But you can provide your own refreshment, and while resting and consuming it, gaze down into the depths of the Nerbudda; it is one of the sacred rivers, and "*sulgramas*" (sacred pebbles) are found in it. The rocks on each side of the stream are at least 200ft. high in some places, and of pure marble; they are seen to the greatest advantage by moonlight. But, by day or by night, they are best observed from a boat; and you can hire one at the place. The rocks, it may be remarked, are infested with monkeys and bees, the latter by far the worse foes of the two. I have not space to linger over the charms of the "marble rocks," but would strongly recommend a rest for a couple of days at Jubbulpore, on purpose to see them. They are well worth a visit, and once seen are not likely to be forgotten.

From Jubbulpore you will most likely run on to Allahabad, which is 229 miles further. This is a large station. One of the best hotels is Kellner's. I speak from past experience;

which may be the best now I do not know, but I believe the one named is still open. Allahabad glories in a variety of public buildings—churches, a college, theatre, garden, baths, hospital, banks, institute, Government offices, a large cantonment, a bazaar, and a handsome and strongly built fort; moreover, the new English suburb of Cannings town, with its wide streets well planted with trees, is becoming quite a considerable place. There are various sights in the vicinity which I can only just mention—the Jumna Masjid, the mausoleum of the Ranee, the fort, in which is the Residency and Akbar's Palace, the Chalee Satoom temple, &c.

The milltary part of the station cantonments is well laid out in fine wide roads, all at right angles, and bordered by beautiful large shady trees. The houses for officers stand separately in squares of ground (compounds), and are some distance apart. The barracks are handsome detached stone buildings of great size, but only hold half a company each. There is also a pretty park, with carefully tended flowers and very fine trees. At Allahabad the Jumna and the Ganges unite, the blue waters of the former mingling with the latter's turbid stream, and the fort stands exactly at the confluence; it was built about 1575 by the Emperor Akbar. This station is generally occupied by about 1000 European soldiers, a regiment of Bengal cavalry, and one of Native infantry. It is the capital of the North-West Provinces, and the Lieutenant Governor has his seat there. We spent a few days here on our way home very agreeably; the society, however, is rather civilian than military, and the station is by no means a favourite one with soldiers.

Cawnpore will probably afford the next break in your journey, unless you go on to Agra; it is 120 miles from Allahabad, and is a flourishing busy place, a very commercial town, with numerous cotton manufactories, flour mills, &c.; it is the seat of the leather trade, Cawnpore saddlery being famous all over India. It is a very dusty place, but popular with sportsmen, as good shooting and pig-sticking are to be had round about. Cholera is a very frequent visitor at Cawnpore, and it is certainly not one of the most healthy stations to remain in. Kellner has an hotel here also, and there are three or four others, besides banks, good bazaars, and shops. The well (of terrible memory) is one of the sights of the place.

From Cawnpore you should run on to Toondla (for Agra),

some 144 miles, and thence to Agra, thirteen miles, where you may well make up your mind, if you can spare the time, to remain for a few days. There are good hotels—Beaumont's, the Railway, and four or five others — but if you have any native servants with you, and a sufficiency of kit, the dâk bungalow, which is prettily situated in a sort of park, will be found very much cheaper. We spent a week there on our way down country, but then we had four native servants with us, and were very comfortable, seeing all the sights, being asked to dine out each night by friends, having a carriage lent us, and so forth; but of course in case of knowing no one in the place, and having no servants engaged, beyond perhaps a bearer, it would be best to go to an hotel and remain there, making excursions at will. Living in an Indian hotel costs about six to eight rupees a day. For this you get four meals at the following times: Tea or coffee at 6 a.m., breakfast at 9 a.m., tiffin at 1 p.m., dinner at 7 p.m.; and with the use of a general sitting room you have a fair sized bedroom. Wines, spirits, beer, soda water, and other liquors other than water are extras.

The chief sight at Agra is, of course, the Taj. It is impossible to enter here into a lengthy description of its features; besides, it needs a pen excelling in the art of word painting to do it any degree of justice; and, even then, words could give but a faint idea of its surpassing beauty. The purity of its marble walls and minarets; the rich mosaics of precious stones, agate, jasper, cornelian, &c., with which it is inlaid; the fretted work, cut out of the solid marble, with which it is everywhere ornamented; and the chaste style of the whole building make up a picture which it is impossible to describe in language adequate to its merits. The Taj is not likely to fade from the memories of those who have visited it. Seen by daylight it is magnificent, by moonlight it is softly beautiful. Perhaps one of the best views of it is to be had from the fort, which is a fine red granite embattled building on the bank of the river Jumna. The Taj Mehal, seen from the higher portion of the fort, is naturally the most conspicuous object visible, as it is the most attractive; when we saw it the setting sun threw a flood of warm light over the pure marble, giving it at first a golden tinge, and then a warmer reddish glow, while the placid waters of the Jumna, gliding smoothly by at our feet, enhanced the beauty of the scene. It would have formed a study for an artist, though the gorgeous tints, if reproduced on canvas, would appear almost too brilliant to be real,

The changes of light and shade towards evening are very varied and rapid in India, so that even whilst we were admiring the lovely view and the warmth and extreme brightness of the colouring, the sun dipped suddenly down, and the wonderful tints we had been revelling in faded as if by magic, the fog rising on the river's banks, and bathing everything in a soft grey mist. It seemed as if a curtain had been lowered over the Taj, so completely was it hidden from our eyes. Within the fort there is much to interest—the throne room, judgment hall, Shah Jehan's palace, Shish Mehal, with its gilded cupolas and wonderful mosaic work, the Pearl Mosque, the Motee Musjid, of the purest white marble, and the Jumna Musjid, with its three domes.

Besides the Taj and the fort there are various places to be visited within a drive—remains of old palaces, gardens, the Rambagh, and mosques. The tomb of Etmatdowlah is well worth seeing, and there are two very handsome tombs on the Secundra-road; but these have been converted into schools. The Taj garden is very pretty, the river adding much to its beauty; but in the attractions of the building itself, one is rather apt to hurry through the garden surrounding it, which is well laid out, and contains shrubs, flowers, grasses, and trees from all parts of the world, and is kept in very good order.

If sufficient time is allowed in Agra, Futtehpore Sikri, the favourite palace of Akbar, ought to be visited. It is very charming, and there is a dâk bungalow there, so that it is possible to spend a few days in this old palace—deserted by man, but a paradise of animal life. The birds seem to look upon it as their own; peacocks, parrots, doves, owls, crows, robins, and smaller birds abound, while the most gaudy butterflies, burnet and hawk moths hover among the flowering shrubs. Hares, too, are numerous, and formerly there was excellent shooting to be had; but probably that is no longer the case. Anyhow, it must be a delightful spot for naturalists to spend a short time in. But I must not linger too long over Agra and its neighbourhood, tempting as it is. Some specimens of soapstone and pietra dura should be bought before leaving. Some of the soapstone boxes are exceedingly pretty and the prices very reasonable—from 3 rupees each, while models of the Taj may be had from 5 rupees, and so on. The plates are also good and well carved, with excellent designs, such as jessamine and mediæval lilies. The soapstone lends itself well to elaborate carving, and some of the touches, especially in the Taj models, are extremely delicate. It is much prized at home, and, if carefully packed, travels well; even if broken, it can be easily cemented together again.

From Agra one must return to Toondla junction, some thirteen miles, in order to join the main line, and go thence towards Lahore, which, however, is rather a long, tedious journey, and might well be broken at Umballa, where there is an excellent dâk bungalow; or at Umritzur, if a visit to the Golden Temple, the chief sight of that place, be wished for.

Lahore is a very large place, the seat of the Lieutenant-Governor, and has many handsome buildings—the Lieutenant-Governor's residence, various Government offices, a college, hospital, museum, gaol, asylum, the Lawrence Memorial buildings, &c. The city itself is very ancient, and was founded between the first and seventh centuries of the Christian era; it has a brick wall seven miles in circumference, and a variety of old ruins — palaces, gardens, temples, tombs, many of them well worth inspection. The Emperor Jehanghir's mausoleum, across the Ravee, should be visited; also the Shalimar Gardens, which are about three miles from the military station of Mean Meer. These contain eighty acres; they are arranged in terraces, and have as many as 450 fountains, most of which, however, are very dilapidated; the trees are very handsome; roses are to be found in great profusion, and there are groves of orange and mango trees. Shalimar is much frequented for picnics in the season, and a very enjoyable day may easily be spent there. We drove down, I remember, from Mean Meer, when we were stationed there, and on another occasion went through the native city of Lahore on an elephant, by far the best and most comfortable way of seeing it, dismounting, of course, at the chief places to be visited.

At Anarkali there is a good club; there is also a handsome tomb to be seen, and there are several good hotels. A few days, too, can be very well spent at Lahore, if time is no great object. The distance thence to Mooltan is 214 miles, chiefly over dreary desert; the journey is best taken by night, as there is little to see save miles on miles of arid desert, relieved by vegetation here and there in the shape of tamarisks, castor-oil plants, and date palms. The Indus Valley railway is now open from Mooltan to Kurrachee, which in my time was not the case. A few more hints before I leave the subject of railway travelling. The engines are fed mostly with wood, so that it is necessary to look out sharply for sparks, which often fly in through the windows. One night we had a railway rug partly burnt from this cause, and if a spark entered while the occupants were asleep the result might be serious. I often wondered why the trains so often made a false start. The engine having set off, it often happens that it is suddenly pulled up with sufficient force to make loosely coupled carriages bump against each other, which, when it goes on at nearly every station, is rather trying to the spine. An air cushion to sit on is, therefore, useful as one of a traveller's "gutree futrees," as small parcels are called.

To those who cannot sleep, the night journeys, as I have said, are very monotonous. The country as you pass through it has, in the moonlight, a weird appearance, which at first interests, but at last palls terribly; the desert which has to be traversed from Lahore to Mooltan appears, under the influence of the moon's soft light, less desolate; it is relieved by scattered palms and tamarisk shrubs, and the long reaches of level sendy plain, looking grey in the moonlight, slip past rapidly. At the stations there is not much to interest; even the bhistie (water carrier), half asleep, is deaf to the calls for water by the natives in the third-class carriages at the far end of the train, and before these have their wants half satisfied the train is off again, with its irritating preliminary bump, bump, and so the night wears on until Mooltan is reached; but tedious as this journey is by night, it is worse by day, the heat, even in the coolest season, with the glare and dust, being intolerable. Mooltan station reached, cantonments are at no great distance; if you have no friends to receive you, the dâk bungalow will be found fairly good, and there you must abide while you search for a house, or, rather, a bungalow.

Mooltan is an ancient city, or at least the native portion, where the fort is situated. It is generally supposed to have been the Malli of Alexander. The fort is a large brick fortress, and has in its enclosure a handsome mosque containing the tomb of Sheik Bahanddeen Zukim, who lived in 1006 A.D. I need not touch here upon the history of the place; it has, however, played a considerable part in great events, especially in the years 1848 and 1849. The citadel, which was once of immense strength, is now much out of repair, and by no means agreeable to be quartered in, with its tiny mud-constructed rooms; the look-out is, however, pretty.

Mooltan boasts a church, hospital, central gaol, barracks, bazaars, banks, gardens, &c. The various bungalows are prettily situated, fine trees are planted along the wide roads, and the date palm (*Phœnix dactylifera*) forms a pleasant feature in the landscape, growing in great abundance all round the neighbourhood. The soil, indeed, is very fertile, not destitute of vegetation even in the hot weather, and amply repaying cultivation.

CHAPTER VIII.

SERVANTS.

First Experiences of Indian Life—Selection of Servants—Necessary Precautions—Masters and Mistresses—Characteristics of Indian Servants—Wages—Variety of Servants and their respective Duties—Further Observations on Indian Servants—Generally Under-rated—Their Good Habits—How to Treat them.

I HAVE mentioned Mooltan particularly, because it was there my experiences of Indian life commenced; but my remarks concerning houses, furnishing, servants, &c., apply pretty much to other parts of the Punjab. Rents and wages differ somewhat in different places, and certain allowances must be made; prices, also, I hear, have risen, since I left India, especially in the matter of servants' wages. I have, therefore, in every case, added a little to the actual cost, in order to allow for the increase.

The selection of a staff of servants I place before the choice of a bungalow, because already on your journey you will probably have engaged one if not two—a bearer and a khitmutgar. It is not advisable to take many servants up country with you, but it is impossible to travel in India with any degree of comfort without at least one; therefore either a bearer or a khitmutgar you must have if you stop at all *en route*, as I have suggested you should do. Immediately on landing at Bombay you will be beset with native servants asking to be engaged, but beware of these obtrusive members of the class, for with many of them solicitation is part of a designing trade; their testimonials are forgeries bought in the bazaars for a trifle, and if you rashly took them into your service, they would only stay with you as long as you remained in Bombay, or Calcutta, or whatever port you might land at, and directly you began your journey up country, abscond with anything they could lay their hands on. These must not be taken as examples of the whole class of native servants; they are scamps who make this proceeding their business, and they try to take in all new comers in the same way. There are thoroughly good servants to be found, as our experience will show.

The servant question is very much the same the world over, and India is no exception to the rule. There are good servants as well as bad, good masters and mistresses, and the reverse. For my part, I believe servants are pretty much what we choose to make them. I am no adherent to the notion that, as a class, servants are good for nothing, though, if we are to judge from complaints heard at home, they are yearly getting worse. I cannot think it, but one thing I do believe—nay, am certain of —namely, that too many masters and mistresses treat servants in an improper way, speak to them as if they were beneath notice, except for fault finding, keep them hard at work, grudge them any little pleasure, refuse them all sympathy, and then expect faithful service, and consider themselves ill-used when, after a brief stay, they are quitted.

This is no highly coloured picture. In most houses nowadays the shortcomings of domestics form the all-engrossing topic of conversation—Jane's and Thomas's delinquencies, cook's impertinence, or "my maid's" insolence or sulkiness—it is always the same, and to many inexpressibly wearisome. The question, too, often greets one, "Do you know of a good cook? mine is so unreliable," &c. "My parlour maid is leaving; do you happen to know one to suit me?" It is certainly true that servants do not remain so long in their places now as they used. Is all the fault really on their side? I question it very much. But what, it may be asked, has all this to do with Indian servants? I answer, much, Indian servants are like English servants. If they are made happy and comfortable, they will be faithful, and often attach themselves to you surprisingly. If they are treated like dogs, cuffed here and kicked there, very naturally they will render you grudging service, will lie, cheat, steal, and circumvent, and think it fair play.

In the matter of servants, you should certainly not allow yourself to be led by the opinion of others. You will be told that natives are everything that is bad and cannot be trusted. Do not rely on hearsay; prove for yourself if it is not a case of giving a dog a bad name. All are not black sheep because some may have been found so. I have seen a good deal of native servants, and I know no reason why, from my experience of them, they should not be trusted quite as much as others of their class.

About ayahs in particular, I have heard most lamentable accounts—what lying, cheating, thieving creatures they were— in short, a "thorough bad lot;" but I know how often in England I had heard the whole class of servants abused, often without rhyme or reason, and so turned rather a deaf ear to my would-be counsellors. I was very particular about my ayah's character, and I saw the lady she had lived with; she was by no means blind to her faults, but still gave her a fair character. She remained with me all the time I was in India, travelled over a thousand miles down country with us to Bombay, and only took leave when we went on board, even coming with us on the ship to see where "missee Baba," my little girl, her especial charge, would sleep, and then shed floods of tears at parting. From that woman I had every possible attention. She was most tender and careful in sickness, nursing me through several severe illnesses; never took the value of a pin's head from me, and would, were I to return to India tomorrow, come back to me, if she were alive, and serve me as faithfully. And all the praise she had from her former mistress was, "Oh! she's a fair ayah, but just like all the rest—will cheat right and left if she has a chance." She had every chance, for we never locked up anything; but, as I said, I never lost the worth of a pin.

She was wonderfully handsome, with well formed features, a fine upright figure, and had the most splendid head of hair I ever saw on any woman; when she stood upright it touched the ground, as it fell around her in waves of raven black; it was not coarse either, but fine as spun silk. It is rather rare to see a native woman's hair, as they generally plait it tight to the head and hide it under their "sarees;" but she let hers down one day, on purpose that I might see how long it was. She had bangles, of course, and anklets; large silver rings on her great toes; one or two very fine roughly set rubies, in rings, on her fingers; and a large turquoise, in a plain gold star-like setting, let into the bone of her nose. So much for "Asmi," and a better maid I never wish to have; gentle, quiet, attentive, careful, and trustworthy—in fact, a domestic treasure.

When she left me I gave her a very good character, which I

considered she deserved. However, in her next place she did not stay much over a month, and I heard afterwards that she was considered stupid, slow, and sulky. So much for difference of opinion.

Our bearer, Seethal, by name, was another specimen of a good native servant; I grant he was a trifle slow, and had a habit of always cleaning the sahib's sword just when wanted for a parade or duty, when it would be all unbuckled, and create delay to put together again. He had been a civilian's servant before he came to us, and it took him some time to learn an officer's ways. He was, however, a most valuable head domestic, thoroughly trustworthy, and kept good order amongst the other servants. We had the highest character with him; he had been through the Mutiny with a former master, a civilian in high position, and had saved his belongings for him when obliged to hide from the fury of the mutineers.

We engaged him at Allahabad on our way up country from Bombay; he remained with us during our stay in India, went down country again to see us off on board the Serapis, "the big white ship," as he called it, and then took service with my brother, with whom he remained until his furlough to England, when the old man—for he was almost an old man when he came to us, and when he left my brother he was really past service—went back to his own home. I had quite a respect for Seethal, and was really sorry to bid him good-bye.

During the Kuka rising, when my husband was obliged to leave me and go out to a camp some miles distant from our station, Seethal used to draw his *charpoy* (wooden and string bed) across my door, and would, I believe, had occasion arisen, have defended my life with his own. As a rule, no native servants — not even the ayahs — sleep in the bungalow, but out in their own houses in the compounds, often scarcely within call. Hence it was by no means part of the old man's duty, and was quite his own idea to constitute himself my guard while the sahib was away.

He was one of the old high caste Hindoos, and I am certain would never prove false to his salt.

Our table servant, or *khitmutgar*, had from boyhood been brought up with the regiment, and knowing my husband—having, in fact, been his servant when he had been in India before, came to us at once. Karéem Bux was his name, and he, too, remained with us as long as we were in the country, and was as honest and trustworthy as the other two.

Of course, we had many other servants, one of the social follies of Indian life being that you must keep three to do the work of one. They were mostly of inferior castes, except the *khánsámán*, or cook; the first we had was certainly a bad servant, that is to say, dishonest, not a bad cook; no Indian cooks are bad so far as their profession goes, they are a race of cooks. This man we soon got rid of, and in his place fortunately obtained a thoroughly good cook and an honest man.

Out of the tribe of coolies, punkah and garden, "grass cuts" and syces, we had only one or two black sheep, whom we were obliged to discharge, and on the whole, we had no reason to complain, especially as all around us we heard grumblings as to the difficulty of obtaining good servants. I begin to believe that grumbling against servants is a national fault amongst us, and one to which we are yearly more prone. In India servants are one of the chief subjects of conversation, but that may be because there are fewer current topics than at home.

With regard to wages and duties, the former are rising each year, even the lower servants requiring higher pay *pro râta* than when we were in India. So I am told by relatives of mine now in the country. Instead, therefore, of copying my old list from "David's Guide," which was a useful book, much in the style of some of Letts's account books, but not now published, I have added some 20 rupees per mensem, reckoning the upper servants as advanced 2 rupees each, and the lower 1 rupee, which ought to allow a fair margin for the present rate of pay:

	R.	A.	P.
Head bearer	10	0	0
Second ditto	9	0	0
Khitmutgar	10	0	0
Ayah	10	0	0
Khánsámán	12	0	0
Dhobie	9	0	0
Mehter	5	0	0
Bheestie	8	0	0
Mallee	8	0	0
Syce	8	0	0
Grass cut	6	0	0
Three punkah coolies (6 rupees each)	18	0	0
Tailor	8	0	0
Rs.	121	0	0

About £12 per mensem, reckoning the rupee at its full value.

The punkah coolies would only be employed during the hot weather, say, for six months. The cost, therefore, of a staff of servants such as I have described would be a little over £135. This seems a large sum to pay for wages only; but it must be remembered these servants do not feed at their master's expense, neither are they found in clothes. Moreover, as probably two bearers would not be required, and the tailor and mallee might be struck off the list, a saving might be effected of some £30 per annum.

Among the list of servants previously given I omitted to mention the familiar chokeydar, or watchman, and the chuprassie, or messenger; but the former is not always kept, neither are messengers, except by those high up in the Civil Service, and the like.

A chokeydar is kept on the principle of "set a thief to catch a thief." We kept one, but beyond the fact of being on duty every night and making a weird noise at stated intervals, I do not see that he was of much use; they say, however, that the mere fact of having one is enough to keep thieves from the house, because they are thieves themselves, and thus turn off the rest of the fraternity. Be this as it may, the old man who prowled around our bungalow, and made night hideous with his unearthly yells, was very feeble, and could not have tackled a robber were it needful, but still he prevented us from being molested. The pay of such a watchman would be about 5 rupees a month.

The duties of the various servants usually employed are much as follows:

The ayah performs all the offices of a lady's maid as well as of a nurse, if there be children. If she were a Portuguese she would probably be able to wash and get up laces, and possibly do a little other work. Mine was a Hindoo, and did nothing beyond an ordinary ayah's duties.

A bearer discharges all the functions of a valet for the sahib; besides which, in the Bengal Presidency, where my experience has chiefly been, he has to look after the other servants, and is, in fact, the butler. To him are usually entrusted articles of value — money, jewels, clothes, &c.; he is also responsible for the plate, and for the general good behaviour of the staff. Generally speaking, he is faithful, and the more trust you put in him the better he will deserve it. I fear the same could hardly be said of all English butlers.

Of course, now and then there are instances of dishonesty, but none came under our notice, for we lost nothing except in the case of the cook before mentioned, who stole some money, and was promptly dismissed.

The khitmutgar's duties are the same as those of a footman or parlourmaid.

The khánsámán is equivalent to an English cook; moreover he will market for you, and for this reason is usually paid house money every day, in order to go out early in the morning and procure the day's provisions.

The syce looks after the horse, but will not cut his grass, which is the "grasscut's" business. The dhobie does nothing but wash your clothes—and tear them! The mehter performs the more menial offices of the establishment. The bheestie carries all the water used in the house, and fills the baths and "gurrahs;" he is usually a high caste man, and can be sent on messages, if a regular chuprassie is not kept.

It is customary to pay servants once a month, and also to keep them at least that time in arrear. This is no real hardship, and should be explained to them as one of your rules when they enter your service. The reason is, that if you pay them up to date you have little or no hold on them, and they may leave you without the least warning, and on the smallest excuse—I allude, of course to new servants; whereas, if you reserve a portion of their wages in your hands, they will not, by leaving suddenly, run the risk of losing it. It is only fair to pay them regularly every month, as in general a native servant has a host of relatives dependent on him.

They are exceedingly kind to their kith and kin, and in this respect set a good example to those who consider themselves far above them in the social scale. I am ready to allow that they have faults—grave ones too—they certainly tell stories, to call them by a mild term, on the smallest provocation, it would seem for the mere delight of telling them; they are regardless of the value of time, and have to be taught to do things when you want them done, not when they think proper, for they seem to fancy that if you order your horse at such a time, an hour sooner or later can make no difference, which, if you are in a hurry, is, to say the least, rather trying. But they can be cured of these faults if you are determined, and insist on your orders being carried out when you wish. Be firm in all your dealings with them, but temper your firmness with kindness, and do not lapse into severity or familiarity; treat them with justice and a certain amount of kindly interest, and you will find they will repay you with cheerful, willing service. If they see that you think of them, and endeavour to make them comfortable and happy, they will become attached to you, and show that they are so by many extra services.

It is the fashion to decry and undervalue native servants, for what reason it would be difficult to say; in nine cases out of ten only from prejudice, or from having heard them disparagingly spoken of by old Anglo-Indians and contemptuously termed "nigs." It would be easy to multiply instances of their fidelity; and far from being unscrupulous, they possess a very high sense of honour—at least, all the best of the race. They have many admirable qualities. On the march they are simply invaluable—no grumbling when told of a long journey in prospect; rarely do they ask for an advance of pay, even when they might reasonably be supposed to want it, and, as for being selfish, I do not believe they know the word. The sahib and mem-sahib are looked after first of all; they are never without troops of relatives dependent on them, and in their own estimation they themselves come last.

It may be thought that I am over-estimating their worth, but I ask any Englishman or woman who really knows India and its people well, if the natives are not habitually undervalued by some of their countrymen? It is taken for granted that they are all that is depraved and bad, and even those who defend them are jeered at and thought poor silly creatures, who will find out the native character some day. I have known instances in which they have been beaten, kicked, had any missile that came to hand thrown at their heads, and been kept without their wages for months; and I ask, is it any wonder that now and then the crushed worm turns, if possible robs his master, and decamps with his property? Treated properly and fairly, Indian servants are quite as good, if not better, than those found in other countries, and if people will only judge for themselves, and refuse to be blinded by prejudice, this they must sooner or later find out, unless they are indeed unfortunate in their selection during the whole time of their stay. *Apropos* of the remarks I made on our old bearer, Seethal, in this chapter, I have since heard that my brother having gone back to India, the old man found him out and returned to his service.

You will not, of course, be able to fall in with all the servants you require at once; but it would be well, before taking possession of your bungalow, to engage the more important—*i.e.*, the bearer, khánsámán, khitmutgar, ayah, mehter, and bheestie. The others you must look out for and procure by degrees. When new comers arrive in a station they are generally soon found out by such servants as are in want of a place. A good plan on first arrival is to inquire if any families are leaving, and if they are parting with their servants. In such a case very good servants are often to be obtained.

After you have examined the chits or testimonials which the natives in search of places bring with them, and you feel inclined to engage them, endeavour, before doing so, to obtain an interview with their previous employers. This, however, is not often to be had, because, generally speaking, they have gone home, or to the hills, and given their servants written characters. If they have not left the country you can possibly obtain by writing all you desire to know. You will more usually, however, have to depend on the written characters, and these, if you engage the holders, should be kept in your own possession to refer to until you part company again, when you, in turn, will have to give a testimonial, unless you have discharged them for some serious fault, in which case they would not ask for a chit. It is naturally a matter of risk to engage a native on his written character only, for it may have been merely borrowed or bought in the bazaar for the occasion, a certain class of persons in India earning their living by dishonestly writing and selling these characters. Again, very often owing to laziness, masters and mistresses are not sufficiently particular in giving a character; though this fault, it must be confessed, is not peculiar to India. In giving chits, a personal description is one remedy against their being stolen or borrowed and used by other persons; and it is also a guide in choosing servants, because, if the description and the personal appearance of the applicant tally, you are not so likely to be deceived; thus, age, height, general personal appearance, condition, and any distinctive marks should all be mentioned as characteristics, by which the holder of the chit may be recognised.

Servants naturally differ a good deal in the three Presidencies; they belong to different races, and are known under different names. In Bombay there are a great many native Portuguese, Hindoos, and Mussulmans, besides a number of Eurasians.

In Calcutta a mixture is found of all the castes and grades in India; and in Madras, besides those named, are a number of native Christians. Give preference to those servants who do not speak much English—they will be found much better, as a rule, than those who do.

In paying wages, make the payments yourself, unless you can thoroughly depend on your bearer to do so; the servants, however, are far better satisfied if paid by the sahib, and besides, pay day is an opportunity for saying a few words of commendation, or the reverse.

CHAPTER IX.

BUNGALOWS.

Rent—Precautions—Native Landlords—External Appearance of the Buildings—Water—Internal Arrangements.

THE rent of a house, or bungalow, as it is called, depends very much on locality, and of course on the size of the building. In towns it is higher than at small stations. For a small bungalow at a large station from 40 to 50 rupees per month would be asked; for one of moderate size, from 60 to 90 rupees; and for extra large buildings, from 300 to 500 rupees per month. These large bungalows are rarely taken except by wealthy civilians or military officers high in the service, who require very large establishments. At up-country stations the rents would be rather lower than those I have named; and for about 80 rupees (£8) you would get a very good-sized bungalow. The accompanying illustration of the ground plan will give an idea of the way in which such houses are built. They have hardly ever upstair accommodation, except in towns, being only one storey high; and the rooms all open into each other and into the verandahs which run round. The pillars supporting the roofs of the verandahs are spanned by arches, and the intervals filled with wide blinds (*chics*) made of bamboo.

It will be seen from this ground plan how many doors there are. They are partly of glass, and therefore muslin blinds are required to stretch across them, and they are also furnished with blinds (*chics*) of reed, which in the hot weather serve for doors, and are as often rolled up as not, but are lowered when it is wished to screen the openings from the verandah. Those doors which open from the outside straight into the living rooms are fitted during the hot weather with mats made of a sweet-smelling grass, *khus-khus* by name, often spelt *cus-cus*, the mats made from it being called "cus-cus tatties," and used for the purpose of cooling the heated atmosphere in dwelling houses during the hot winds. They are fitted to those doors facing the direction of the wind, and are kept wet by means of water

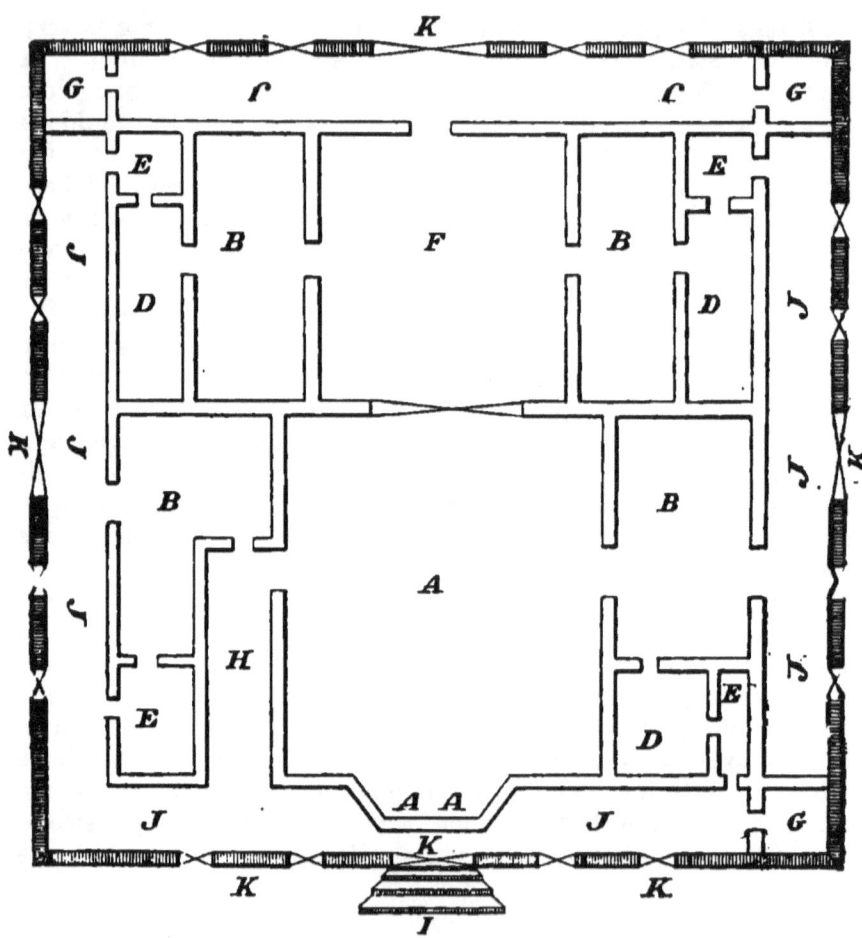

GROUND PLAN OF BUNGALOW.

A—Drawing-room. *AA*—Bay Window. *B*—Bedrooms. *D*—Dressing-rooms. *E*—Bathrooms. *F*—Dining-room. *G*—Godowns. *H*—Hall. *I*—Chic Entrance. *J*—Verandahs. *K*—Arches on Verandahs.

dashed on them from outside, the hot air which is drawn through them by the action of the punkah being cooled by passing through the wet grass.

To return to the general subject: £7 or £8 a month seems a good deal to pay for rent, for the exterior of the building is rarely agreeable to the eye—a square mud house, badly painted outside, and in colours which would make the æsthetic shudder—bright yellow, glaring white—no sweet subdued low-toned tints, but all harsh and crude. Within the bare walls there is plenty of scope for decorative ideas and artistic ornamentation, but the Indian climate is scarcely one in which to indulge fads and fancies, if they have to be carried out by the originator.

In the choice of a bungalow there are several things to be considered, unless the station in which you find yourself be deficient in houses, in which case you may have to put up with what you can get. In the first place, the situation should be high and tolerably open. A few trees are an advantage in a compound, but too many are the reverse, because they keep off the air from the house. The huts of the native servants should never be too near, and I should reject any bungalow which had this disadvantage. There should be a large deep well in the compound in perfect repair, and containing a good supply of water. Have some drawn up to taste, and test it with your pocket filter. Good water is a *sine quâ non* everywhere; in India especially you should be sure of having it good, and enough of it for all purposes, both for house requirements and for the garden, if you cultivate it, as I should most strongly advise you to do if you remain some time in one station.

External arrangements first seen to, you should narrowly inspect the interior of the building. If it wants white-washing or re-staining have it done before you enter on possession, or you will find life a burden from insects of various unpleasant kinds. See that the walls are quite firm and dry, that the beams and woodwork are not eaten by white ants, and choose a house with the rafters of the roof visible rather than one which has a canvas ceiling, for if this latter is the case you will run the danger of being disturbed by rats, squirrels, and the like. The space between roof and ceiling is a favourite retreat of animals and birds, and they will make night sleepless by their various cries and frolicsome gambols overhead. This will, in a certain measure, be the case even with an open roof, but then you can hunt the enemy out, which otherwise you could not.

Keep your landlord very strictly to any terms you may make

with respect to the alterations or repairs which you wish done. Before you enter your new abode—supposing you have found one you like—refuse to sign any document until he has done all he promised, and then see that the conditions respecting rent, repairs, &c., are most particularly and carefully stated, and have your signature witnessed by three, or at least two witnesses. So many disputes and misunderstandings arise on such subjects, more especially with native landlords, that one cannot be too careful. In one instance I remember ours was a native landlord, and was most tiresome about repairs. Time was of no account with him, and he once told my husband, when remonstrating with him, "that he expected things done as with a magic wand." He was Parsee and spoke English. The well was one great source of discomfort to us, as he would not keep it in good repair; and we had not looked quite as narrowly after it as we ought to have done when taking the bungalow. I mention this as a hint that others may learn to be more particular than we were.

CHAPTER X.

FURNISHING.

Carpets—Matting—White Ants—Their Destructiveness—Prevention—Scinde Rugs—Hangings—Furniture and Fittings—Anglo-Indian Furniture Sales—A Catalogue of Requirements—General Domestic Appointments.

WHEN you have finally decided on your house, you must see about the chics and matting for the arches, windows, and floors, for these are the first things required. Measure the arches of the verandah for the large chics, and the doors of the rooms for the small and finer kind. Neither sort is expensive, the former costing from 8 annas (1s.) to 1 rupee 8 annas (3s.) each, and the latter from 8 annas to 1 rupee each.

The rooms are never floored, as white ants would soon destroy boards. The flooring is made of mud, well baked (*chunam*). This makes a hard smooth surface when well laid, and is easily kept clean by sweeping. Two kinds of matting are usually spread over the rooms; one, the uppermost, of fine China kind, the other, beneath it, of a coarser description. Where carpets are laid down, as in drawing and dining rooms, the finer matting can be dispensed with, but in its place a coarse cloth, previously soaked in a solution of corrosive sublimate in the proportion of 1lb. to three gallons of water, should be laid beneath the carpet or *dhurrie*, as this will prevent the white ants, sworn enemies to carpets, from destroying it. If the cloth is dyed with indigo it will have the same effect. The matting for an ordinary sized house will cost from 60 to 80 rupees, that is if you have two kinds—one on top of the other. We contented ourselves with one sort, if I remember aright, and had dhurries in the drawing room and dining room. Bedrooms and dressing rooms should be matted all over with rugs in front of dressing tables and beds.

Our rugs were of the kind thought so much of in England now —Scinde rugs. It is a great mistake to carpet a bedroom. Rugs you can have moved and shaken daily, and thus be sure they are not hiding places for insects.

The carpets which are made in the gaols are the most useful, and wear very well. Their price varies with size—from 20 to 60 rupees would be the general price for gaol dhurries. They are made in squares, the ends finished off with fringe, and are generally woven in stripes, indigo blues, greys, or browns, relieved with very narrow red or orange stripes, not bright colours by any means, but agreeably low toned. These common dhurries have no pattern, like the more expensive "oriental" carpets, and are only meant for rough wear. Yet they are not unornamental, the colours being always in good taste.

If, while in India, you chance to light on a carpet of really good old Indian design, unless it is very expensive, and beyond your means, purchase it at once. Look on it in the light of an investment, and bring it home with you. Unfortunately, we English are spoiling the Indian carpet industry. The old low-toned tints, worked in exquisitely artistic designs, are being superseded by bright glaring colours; aniline dyes are creeping in, and such horrors as magenta, vivid greens, crude blues, &c., appear now in most Indian stuffs. Far from improving on Eastern colours and taste, we are rapidly doing our best to ruin both.

When you have put up the chics and put down the matting and dhurries, then your bungalow will begin to look a little ship-shape, though still very empty and bare. Some say eschew curtains of all kinds, even in your drawing room and dining room; but with this I cannot agree, for, without them, your rooms can never look cosy or inhabitable. I hold this view as far as bedrooms are concerned, as there I think they are unnecessary; but, if you do not drape the high door-like windows of the chief rooms in the house, you will never get rid of the comfortless unfurnished look.

We had chintz curtains and lace, which we took out from England with us. I advised, in a former chapter, those married people intending to settle in India for some time to do the same. I will suppose that the advice was followed, and that you have chintz or cretonne sufficient for curtains and coverings. These you can get made up by a durzee, who will sit in your verandah and work all day under your direction. In India you can buy basketwork chairs and sofas very reasonably, and these, wadded with *ruhi* (cotton), covered with a coarse sort of cotton cloth first of all, and then with the chintz, make very good easy lounges. You will also have your deck chairs and cushions you brought out for use on the voyage; and if you are fortunate, and there is a sale going on in the station soon after your arrival, you will be able to pick up such necessary articles as ordinary chairs, tables of various kinds, beds, almirahs (wardrobes), &c. Nearly all these things, with the exception of the beds, will be made of toon wood, which is very serviceable for furniture. The tree from which it is obtained is called *cedrela toona*, and grows to some 60ft. in height. The timber is very like mahogany—indeed, it is often called Indian mahogany; it is, however, lighter in colour and not so close in the grain, though still a close-grained, dense, hard red wood; it takes a very high polish, and is valuable in India because it is not subjected to worms, does not warp, and is very durable. It grows in dry deciduous forests up to 4000ft. elevation, and is known by the natives in different parts of India under different names. The colour improves much with age. When new it is rather too red, but frequent polishing and rubbing removes this fault. A good strong toon wood table will have seen the inside of most of the houses in a station probably before you become its possessor, for people never dream of taking their furniture with them from place to place as we do at home. Before one station is left for another, all bulky articles are sold off without reserve; the owner makes out a list of what he intends to sell, puts what he considers a fair price on each article, and sends the list by a chuprassie the round of the station. Those who see the list and fancy anything mentioned in it, write their names against it, and pay the price for it when it is given over.

This simple method of selling off furniture holds good in most Indian stations; the things change owners with very little trouble, and in most cases at fair prices. In the case of English goods, glass, china, and the like, the full value is very nearly always fetched, so that before your return home, you can count on disposing of all the articles you brought out that you do not wish to keep. In buying before starting for India, this fact should be borne in mind, and your numerous purchases looked on in the light of investments, for which you will be able to recoup yourself in the end.

I have now by me our list of sale, with the prices the things fetched when we sold them off, and I have been able to give many hints on these and similar matters to people going out who have asked my advice.

The following would be fair prices to give in buying when furnishing your house :—

	Rup.	An.
A drawing-room round table, toon wood, of course	20	0
A large easy chair, toon wood	10	0
Ordinary chairs (each)	4	0
Small easy chairs (wicker work) (each)	5	0
Sofa or lounge chair	15	0
Fair size dhurrie	35	0
Smaller dhurrie	20	0
Small table (5 o'clock tea) (each)	6	0
Side table	12	0
Dining table	20	0
Almirah (wardrobe) (large)	25	0
Almirah (wardrobe) (small)	15	0
Folding screen	20	0
Dressing table	10	0
Cane chairs (each)	3	0
Bed with poles, mosquito curtains, &c.	20	0
Small ditto	15	0
Washstand (complete)	18	0
Small ditto	12	0
Towel horse	2	0
Large looking glass	10	0
Small ditto	6	0
Bath (wood)	8	0
Commode	8	0
Tattie tub	1	0
Ice box	8	0
Meat safe	6	0
Filter stand	3	0
Kitchen table	6	0
Set of dechsies (cooking pots)	25	0
Oven	5	0
Kettle	5	0
Pestle and mortar	3	0
Spit	0	8
Spoon	0	8
Knife	1	0
Frying-pan	2	0
Chopper	0	8
Pantry table	4	0
Dhobie's table	4	0
Gauffring irons	1	8
Common stools (to be covered), each	0	8
Hand punkah	3	0

Saddle stand	4	0
Water jars (large), each	1	0
Ditto small, each	0	8
Mats for bath room, each	2	0
Square of cocoa-nut matting	5	0

Our furniture, with chics, tatties, matting, &c., cost us a little over 600 rupees (£60), but then we did not furnish all the rooms in the bungalow, and took out curtains and coverings of various kinds with us, glass, china, plate, &c.

The punkahs spoil the look of any room, but they are necessary evils, and if you wish to be at all comfortable in the hot weather, must be put up with. The vallance is put on full, and is made of some white or écru washing material; it can be edged with a bind of the colour prevailing in the room, which, I think, should be a low-toned green, as affording most rest to the eye. Punkahs are provided by the landlords of all bungalows, and are his property; he provides also the cords, but the vallances you must furnish yourself. By dint of hanging up photographs, pictures, brackets for odds and ends of china, Japanese scrolls, having books and papers about, and a piano, which you can hire in most stations, a room can be made fairly pretty. A bright rug or two here and there, either on the matting or dhurrie; a covered mantelpiece board, with lace or crewel worked border, and a glass in a plain velvet setting above it, with a few quaint ornaments about, will add much to the habitable look of an Indian room. But in hanging all pictures, scrolls, velvet covered brackets, or the glass above mentioned, let them stand out from the wall, so as not to touch it, for if they do the white ants will assuredly make a meal off them. Crewel-worked cloths which are washable, for the tables, and coverings for the sofa and chair cushions, also give a more finished look to a room.

In many cases the drawing and dining rooms are only divided by a wide arch, which requires to be fitted up either by a large folding screen or a *purdah* (curtain) hung by rings on a pole.

It is also usual to have purdahs hung over all the doors which open from the bedrooms into the drawing and dining rooms. These look well when they match the window curtains and coverings. In choosing cretonne or chintz for this purpose (it would have to be lined to make it thick enough), I should give the preference to an oriental sort of pattern, which would look rich without being too hot or heavy; have it not too light in colour, or it will become dirty too soon. Lace curtains will relieve the look of rather dark colours, and really, in India, the darker your rooms are, in reason, the more cool and comfortable they are to the inmates.

A square of matting, strongly bound, or a small dhurrie, will be found very useful for taking out in the compound, to spread on the ground underneath your chairs, in the evenings when you sit out to take your after dinner coffee. It is also very useful on the march.

CHAPTER XI.

HOUSEKEEPING.

Cost of Living—General Augmentation of Prices—Diminution of Salaries—Increase of Luxury—English Equivalents of Indian Currency—Weights and Measures—Choice of Food —Marketing—Butchers' Meat—" Mutton Clubs"—Native Cooking—Kitchen Expenses.

THE cost of living in India has increased considerably of late years, and is still increasing, especially in the large towns, Bombay, Calcutta, Madras, &c. Numerous causes go to account for the increase, and the consequences to Europeans in India are decidedly serious.

The competition of the nineteenth century makes the struggle to exist much harder than in days gone by. We do not now hear of "fat fortunes" being made in a few years, and of men returning to their native country to spend the wealth they have amassed. In these days there are far too many candidates in the field for fortune making, and India is for the English no longer the El Dorado it once was.

Eurasians and educated natives now compete with Europeans for vacant offices, and the salaries for coveted berths are lowered by the fact that skilled labour is cheaper—I include mental and brain work under the general head of labour. The market for this sort of ware is becoming almost as glutted in India as at home, and even to the man clever in his profession—I am not now alluding to the Services—there is considerable difficulty in obtaining good appointments.

It is so easy, comparatively speaking, to take a run home to England to refresh the enfeebled constitution, and then go out again, that the climate is not looked on with the dread it once was. Consequently men flock out from England, and for every Englishman in India in the old days, when it took many months

F

to get there, ten or more, I venture to say, might now be found. And what does this mean but the same race for any vacant appointment as goes on at home, the same fight for place or living, and with very often the same result—disappointment?

Salaries which forty or fifty years ago would have provided well for the men receiving them are now insufficient—for family men, at least. The cost of living has increased; it is the fashion for wives to "go to the Hills," even if their health does not really require the change; the native servants ask more wages; that bugbear to the Englishman, *dustoor*, in other words, custom, adds to the expenses of Europeans, while filling the pockets of natives, dealers and servants alike, and housekeeping is thereby rendered a more difficult task than ever. It therefore behoves everyone, especially on first settling in India, to be careful in the way of commencing living.

As a preliminary duty, the comparative values of the silver and copper coinage should be thoroughly well learnt. Do not start with an idea that because the rupee is equivalent to 2s. it will really go as far as that sum would at home. That is a fallacy of which the sooner you disabuse your mind the better.

The following table of the equivalents of Indian money may be found useful. The standard currency of continental India consists of silver. There is hardly a gold coin in circulation; now and then a gold *mohur* is met with, but it is looked on rather as a curiosity. It is worth 16 rupees, or 32s., and weighs 180gr. Troy. There are also gold coins called *pagodas* and *fanams* in the southern provinces, but they are very rarely seen out of collections.

The standard coin of British India is the silver rupee. It is the legal medium of circulation, but its exchange value varies with the money market. Some twenty-five years ago it rose above 2s., but it has decreased since then, with fluctuations, being as low in 1878-9 as 1s. 9d. The copper coins are the *anna*, the *pice*, and the *pie;* and the silver, the 4-anna piece, or ¼ of a rupee, the 8-anna piece, or ½ of a rupee, and the rupee itself. Thus:—

	£	s.	d.
1 pie	0	0	0¼
3 pie (1 pice)	0	0	0¾
4 pice (1 anna)	0	0	1½
4 annas (¼ rupee)	0	0	6
8 annas (½ rupee)	0	1	0
16 annas (1 rupee) ....at par	0	2	0
1 lakh (100,000 rupees)	10,000	0	0
1 crore (100 lakhs)	1,000,000	0	0

There is also a paper currency (authorised) for sums of 5 rupees upwards to 10,000 rupees. Notes are issued from the head offices in Bombay, Calcutta, Madras, and in some of the large cities, as Lahore, Allahabad, Kurrachee, Nagpore, &c.

Having mastered the coinage, you must acquaint yourself with the tables of weights and measures, as you will find such knowledge useful in giving out stores and in the culinary department generally. When I was in India, a very useful diary was published quarterly, called "David's Household and Commercial Guide," which contained a great deal of valuable information. I wrote for one last year, but found they were no longer published, and I do not know if any other kind have taken their place. They gave all the tables which such books usually do, and for housekeepers, especially new comers, were useful acquisitions. I extract from an old one the

BAZAAR WEIGHT.

4 Siki or quarters make 1 Tolah.
5 Tolahs make 1 Chittack.
4 Chittacks make 1 Pauwa.
4 Pauwas make 1 Seer.
5 Seers make 1 Passeri.
8 Passeries or 40 Seers make 1 Maund.

The bazaar seer = 2lb. 0oz. 13dr. The factory seer = 1lb. 13oz. 14dr. A maund of oil would be sixteen bottles, 82lb. going to what is termed a bazaar maund; a factory maund is less, about 74lb. 11oz.

Meal, charcoal, vegetables, fish, ghee, sugar, brass and copper goods are all sold by the *seer;* hay and grass by the *pullah* (dry measure).

Accounts should be very strictly kept, even more so, if possible, than at home. I settled my khánsámán's bill each day; some people do this weekly, but it is impossible to check off the items correctly, at least so I found, unless I made it a daily business, and when once I got into the way it really took but little time. I never gave the man the money to expend, but made him get the things and pay for them himself, paying him again. Thus at night he came in for the mem-sahib's orders for next day, and then he could start off as early as he liked to the bazaar and make his purchases. After breakfast he appeared in the drawing room neatly dressed in his white *cupras* (clothes), bringing his bill for the preceding day; this

I checked off, entering each item in my book, and paying for the whole. At first I found it irksome, knowing so little of the language, and not being able to make out what the man meant, but, in time, it became easy enough, and practice makes perfect.

You can keep a good check on the price of the various articles the man buys by comparing the prices he charges you with those of the monthly "bazaar tariff," a copy of which you must provide yourself with. The prices ruling in the bazaar are fixed by the master of it and by the magistrate of the station, so that by comparing the list with your bills you will soon see if your man is endeavouring to cheat you or not.

Meat is very bad in India—I mean beef and mutton. To obtain the latter good, the only plan is to belong to a "mutton club." Bread is best obtained, if you are military, at the commissariat, being that which is served out to the soldiers. The same may be said of the meat. Vegetables are cheap and plentiful, and, if you do not cultivate a bit of garden, they can be procured without much trouble; so with game, fish of various kinds, and fruit. It is tolerably easy to make out a bill of fare, except in the very height of the hot weather, when nothing will keep good; these are the sad times for housekeepers who know not how to vary the diet or tempt the jaded appetite, which literally revolts at the sight of fresh meat—really fresh meat—for you must eat it the same day it is killed, or not at all.

The kitchen in India is always some little distance from the house; it is usual to visit it once a day to see that all is as it should be, that the *báwarchi-khána* has been swept and garnished, and that the cooking utensils (*dechsies*) are clean and bright. These will require to be re-tinned inside at least once a month, as, being of copper, it would be dangerous to leave them longer. From 12 annas to 2 rupees would be the charge for performing this operation, according to the number of the pots and pans to be done, but sometimes as much as 2 rupees 8 annas is charged for an extra quantity. After the morning visit to your kitchen it is not usual to go out again to it during the day. The native ways are not as our ways, and the less you see of them over their cooking operations the more appetite you will have for the food set before you. They are very good cooks; excellent dishes of all kinds they can produce—made dishes, sweets, cakes, &c.; only do not be too curious as to the ways and means by which the result is attained. The dish may be so nice that you would like to know exactly how it is made. Get your khánsámán to tell you how he prepares it, and write down the ingredients and quantities of each as he names them; this is how I used to do; but never mind overlooking him at his work. Let the fact that it is done, and well done, suffice, or you may never again care to look at that particular dainty. Natives' ways in cooking are not by any means nice, in fact, very often extremely nasty; therefore do not seek to know too much.

CHAPTER XII.

EATING AND DRINKING.

Family Means—General Remarks—Variation of Fare—Wines and other Drinks—Warning against Stimulants—Danger from Unfiltered Water—The Delhi Boil—Importance of the Indian Morning Meal—Indian Tea, Coffee, and Dairy Produce—Preparation—Dishes.

I WOULD advise all housekeepers in India to furnish themselves at first with a blank book, in which to enter the breakfasts, luncheons, and dinners they order on one side, and the price of each item opposite.

By this means not only can you avoid having the same dishes for each meal too frequently, but you will know what each dish costs, and how much the day's expenditure ought to be. You will also have merely to glance at your book if in doubt what to have. I do not mean, of course, that you will do this every day of your life, but for a few months or so, and then afterwards add any new dishes your khánsámán makes, or your menus for your dinner parties, if you have them.

In India you have, during the hot weather more especially, plenty of time, and the more you employ yourself in housekeeping matters the less long the days will seem. Moreover, you will in after years, when you are home again, have your books to turn to, and from them be able to help any of your friends who may be going out, or answer questions relative to India asked in papers. I have found my rough note books of the greatest service to me in many ways.

I give one or two dinner menus from them; these are not for dinner parties, but only the ordinary bills of fare just for a married couple and perhaps a friend—for friends very often drop in to dinner in India "quite promiscuously," especially bachelor friends.

MENU I.

First Course.

Soup.   Green Peas (*Belatee mutter*).
Small hump of beef (boiled).
Vegetables—Potato (*Aloo*) chips.
Borecole.

Second Course.

Teal (*Sulee*) Roasted.
Mango-fool.   Cheese straws.

Dessert.

Any fruit in season.
Coffee.

The cost of this dinner would be about 2r. 6a., including the purchase of vegetables, supposing you have no garden, together with peas for the soup. These should be fresh, not tinned:

	R.	A.
Vegetables	0	6
Beef	1	0
Teal	0	4
Mangoes	0	2
Limes	0	1
Milk	0	2
Butter	0	1
Dessert	0	6
	2	6

Here is another family menu:

MENU II.

First Course.

Fish (*mutchlee*) Chilwars.

(These are small fish not unlike our whitebait; they are fried on sticks, about a dozen or so on one stick, and should be fried a light brown colour. They are not taken off the sticks to serve, but sent up on them, and fresh green limes and very thin bread and butter brought to table with them).

Small shoulder or leg of gram-fed mutton.
Vegetables (*subjee*), potato balls, cauliflowers (*fool kobee*).

SECOND COURSE.

Quails (*butter*).

(Roasted they are best stuffed with green chillies, wrapped in vine leaves, and served with a good clear gravy and fresh green limes. Some people like bread sauce with them).

Dates and Custard.

(This is a dish I never met with anywhere, so I suppose I may lay claim to its invention. Stone and wash some fresh and quite ripe dates; bruise them until they become pulpy; then lay them in the bottom of a glass dish, and pour over them a rich custard. Eaten when quite cold, this is a very good dish for a family party, and, if ornamented with blanched almonds, cut into narrow strips, is quite presentable for any occasion).

Cheese Fondu.

Dessert and coffee.

The cost of this dinner would be 3r., or rather more, say 3r. 6a., thus:

	R.	A.
Fish	0	4
Mutton (if gram fed)	1	8
Quail	0	4
Vegetables	0	4
Dates	0	2
Eggs	0	2
Milk	0	2
Butter	0	2
Cheese	0	2
Limes	0	1
Chillies	0	1
Dessert	0	6
	3	6

MENU III.

Vegetable marrow (*dill pussund*) soup.
Curried mutton.
(An Indian cook's idea of curry is very different from that of an English cook's).
Boiled fowl and mushroom sauce.
Mashed potatoes.   Brinjals.
Almond puffs.
Cheese toast.
Dessert.   Coffee.

Cost about 2r., thus:

	R.	A.
Vegetables, including vegetable marrow for soup...	0	6
Curry	0	4
Fowl	0	6
Almonds	0	4
Cheese	0	2
Eggs	0	2
Milk	0	2
Butter	0	2
Dessert	0	4
	2	0

It is comparatively easy to vary these menus each day in the cold season, but when the hot weather sets in it becomes a matter of considerable difficulty. Then, however, people have no great appetites, and the breakfast is the best meal—not the *chota hazaree*, or small early breakfast, taken just before you ride, or when you return from it as the case may be, but the more substantial one about nine or ten o'clock, to which your friends often drop in, your gentlemen friends more especially. In the hot weather this is the meal to exercise your talents on, and I intend to devote considerable space to it; fish, omelets, new ways of dressing eggs, cunningly-contrived toasts, fresh fruits, and so on, should be plentifully provided for; as a rule, in the hot weather, this is the one repast eaten with appetite during the whole day. Luncheon becomes wearisome, five o'clock tea bores you, and late dinner is a positive *gêne;* but a hearty breakfast you can often—indeed, generally do—eat if appetising viands are provided.

To do this meal full justice, however, you must not rise direct from your bed to partake of it, but come in fresh from your morning ride, if you are a lady; from your military or civilian duties, if you are a man. The heat of the climate is apt enough to produce laziness, lassitude, and *ennui*, and the fight against its enervating influence is by no means a light one; but those who do so fight gain a substantial reward—health. There is plenty to do, even in India, in the hot weather, if people would only believe it, and believe also that employing the mind, if it is too hot to employ the body actively, is the one way of getting through a hot season with any degree of comfort to themselves or those around them. Read, make notes of what you read, write if you can, or draw; work is more difficult to accomplish.

because your hands and your needle alike suffer from the extreme heat; keep your accounts also, amuse yourself by planning fresh dishes for your table, do anything as long as you do not give in and go to bed to sleep, because if you do that you are nearly certain to end by being ill, and becoming a nuisance not only to yourself, but to your friends.

I have not yet spoken of wines or other drinks of any sort. Really, this is the expensive part of Indian living. It is undoubtedly a thirsty country—very thirsty; but you must learn to quench your thirst with drinks of a non-stimulating nature, that is, if you wish to keep your health. I do not say that wine in moderation, and now and then brandy, very much qualified, may not be taken—indeed, in many cases they are necessary—only they must not be abused. Too many people, young men more especially, take a "peg"—a mixture of brandy and soda water—on all occasions, which it is unnecessary to say, is a very bad habit. Soda water, if taken in large quantities, is a decidedly lowering drink; brandy taken when it is not really required is worse than lowering in the Indian climate—it is downright injurious. If malt liquor suits, "hill beer," brewed in the hills, is a very good beverage. It is not so strong as English beer, nor so heavy, and by no means so expensive. Very much more is now brewed in the country than formerly, and the art of brewing is much better understood. There are now as many as nineteen breweries in India, five in the Punjab, five in the North-west Provinces, one in Bombay, three in Madras, two in Mysore, and three in Burmah. In 1879 these produced in all 1,569,026 gallons of ale, beer, and porter, and last year it is said there was a considerable increase.

Iced tea and coffee, fresh lime juice and water, are also favourite drinks, especially with ladies; the two former are very good for a day's shooting; but there would be little use in icing them, as they would soon get warm, unless ice were taken on the expedition. Water is hardly ever good in India, and great care should be exercised in drinking it. It requires to be not only filtered but boiled before filtering, and, though this may sound very fussy, still, believe me, it is necessary. Indian water is filled with organic life; all water is to a certain extent; but the water in India is most impure, and, if used for drinking without going through the necessary processes of boiling and filtering, affects in some mysterious way the whole system, and produces boils and sores of every description. One disease in particular, the "Delhi boil," which arises from drinking bad water, I have had sad experience of, as my husband was invalided twice from this cause alone. He was left in the Terai one night by his bearers, who dropped his dhoolie and ran away, and he had to drink bad water or none, the store he had taken with him being exhausted. The result of this was not felt until some time afterwards, when a "Delhi boil" developed itself, and he had to be sent home, as leaving the country is supposed to be the only effectual remedy. It is curious that once the system has suffered from this cause, the disease appears to have so thoroughly penetrated it that the germs are left, and on a return to the country the boil manifests itself afresh. Such was the case in this instance. On the patient's return to India, after the lapse of nearly twelve months, the disease broke out again, and the same remedy of sending home had to be adopted.

It is, therefore, absolutely necessary that all drinking water should be thoroughly purified before use. Some of the small sized filters are very good for use at table, in bedrooms, and so on; and as they are not always to be obtained in the country, they should be taken out with you.

The early morning is undoubtedly the pleasantest time of the day in India—at least, those find it so who are active and energetic by nature, and like getting up early. The air is then fresh and pleasant, that is from, say, 4 a.m. to 7 a.m., by which time the sun (in the hot weather) has commenced to assert his power rather unpleasantly, and you beat a retreat before him.

It is not easy to turn out every morning at the early hour I name; but look on it as a duty, and persevere in the practice, and it soon becomes a regular habit which you would not like to break off.

An early cup of tea, or glass of milk, and a biscuit or two, taken while you are dressing, and you are ready when you quit your dressing room to get on your pony and canter off into the country. This is the time for exploring, for wandering through the fields, looking at the various crops, discovering new roads and pretty little bits of rural life, making sketches of old mosques, tombs, and the like—possibly seeing the troops manœuvre on the *maidan* (plain), or taking *chota hazari* with your friends at a little distance. The morning is the only time, while the hot weather lasts, in which you feel capable of any decided exertion, and it is certainly the only time in which you thoroughly enjoy your life. Your ride, or drive (if you do not affect exercise on horseback) over, you come back to breakfast, finishing your toilet before that time, and having the refreshment of a cold water bath after your exertions.

Breakfast is a meal to which very often an intimate friend or two will be invited. Brother officers of your husband (if he is a military man) will often drop in, sometimes without invitation (when they anticipate a welcome) after parade; so it is well to make rather a study of the meal, and have it served in as appetising a way as possible. In India you will of course drink the tea of the country, and the coffee also. The latter you will always get green and roast yourself; the natives make it very well, clear, and strong. It is very rarely you are offered the sort of coffee which is too often set before you at home—thick, sloppy, and weak. As for tea, very soon Indian tea will be much more drunk than it is now in England, as also in Australia and America, and most certainly in India itself; its merits only require to be better known to insure its steady sale, and the demand for it is rapidly increasing every year. Few people who have once given Indian tea a fair trial go back to Chinese, because it is really purer and less expensive, in that a smaller quantity is required, for, being stronger, it goes much further. You will generally find Anglo-Indians, when at home again, drink Indian tea by preference. We do, and I know many others who do likewise.

I will say, then, that you are certain of having good tea and coffee. Indian sugar is of an inferior quality generally, because the methods of manufacturing it from the sugar cane are still crude and imperfect. The sugar cane (*Saccharum officinarum*) grows perfectly in India—which is, indeed, the home of the cane; but though its uses have been known from very early times, very little advance has been made in the art of refining. Some day we may hope to see this state of things altered, that is, when European capital and skill in manufacture are brought to bear on the article.

Milk is an article which in India is not always good. However, even if you do not keep milch cows, as many do, you can see that it is not watered, by having the cows, if you buy the milk, brought to your own door, and milked there. Even then the people in charge of the animals will, if you do not yourself see that the *lotahs* (vessels) brought to hold the milk are quite empty before the process begins, put water into them, and so adulterate the milk. When it is brought into the house it should be kept in a cool place, where there is a current of air (an empty room answers very well if you have no regular dairy), and wire screens should be kept over the milk pans, to prevent insects, flies, ants, &c., getting into them. Before you set the milk for cream, the pan containing it should be dipped in cold water, and the cream should be skimmed off before the milk is at all sour, if it is wanted for use at table.

Butter is made by the natives in a very primitive manner—by shaking the cream in a bottle until it turns to butter. If you, however, wish to have it good, you must use a churn, and when the butter is taken away it must be placed on a sloping board, so that the buttermilk may run off. After this it should be pressed, beaten, rolled, and sprinkled with salt, again pressed, until there is no more moisture left in it and it is quite firm, when it can be shaped for use. It should be kept in a porous dish, with damp cloths around it, and in a current of air. A good way to preserve it sweet while on the march or travelling by rail, is, when it has been thoroughly pressed and is quite firm, to mix with it some black peppercorns which have been washed and dried, and then put it into a *chattie* or jar and place on the top some moist sugar laid between two folds of linen. Preserved like this it keeps for many days.

Clotted Cream can be quickly made in this manner : Let the milk stand for four hours, then simmer it very gently over a charcoal fire, remove it before it begins to boil, and put the pan on the shelf on which you mean it to remain, but it must not be shaken in the moving. The cream which rises on the pan will be fit for use in about twelve hours. If wanted for butter it must stand twenty-four hours, and then, if skimmed with care and shaken in a wide-mouthed glass bottle, the butter comes very quickly.

Eggs (*undah*), dressed in various ways, are certain to appear on all breakfast tables. Besides the more simple ways of preparing, such as boiling, poaching, and frying, the natives cook them in many ways, such as—

Buttered eggs, commonly called by the natives "rumble tumble." This dish is made thus : Beat from four to ten eggs, according to the amount you wish to make, strain them carefully, put some butter into a saucepan over the fire, with salt to taste, turn it one way until it is melted, then put into it your beaten eggs, and stir them round until they are quite thick, only do not allow the mixture to curdle. Have ready some bits of buttered toast, keep them warm before the fire, pour the egg mixture on to them, and serve very hot. Green chillies, very finely minced up, are often added to a "rumble tumble," and are a great improvement.

Brouillés.—Take six eggs and beat the yolks and whites together with pepper and salt to taste. Put them in a stewpan over the fire (not too fierce a one), and stir continually, that the mixture may be quite smooth. A wooden spoon is the best to use for this. Add a tablespoonful of good white broth, and the articles you mean to put in the mixture—mushrooms, asparagus heads, or artichokes.

Buttered Eggs and Broccoli.—Wash and clean the broccoli, removing the stalk and leaves, cut it into quarters, and boil it in salt and water; beat four eggs well, put them into a saucepan in which 3oz. of butter have been melted, with a little salt, over the fire. The eggs should be put in when the butter is warm, and the mixture should be shaken until it is thick. Prepare a toast, which set quite hot in the centre of a dish; pour the eggs on to it, and garnish with the broccoli.

Surprise Eggs.—Boil eight eggs quite hard, cut them into halves and take out the yolks, put them into a mortar with two tablespoonfuls of butter, and pound well together, adding a little cream, pepper, salt, and grated nutmeg, also one raw egg to make it bind. Take the whites and pare them out thin, fill one half of the eggs with the pounded mixture and the other halves with chopped parsley, some finely cut up green chillies, and some more of the mixture. Heap up what is left of the pounded egg in the centre of the dish and garnish all round with the stuffed eggs, put into the oven for about ten minutes, and serve very hot. This makes a very good dish, pretty and appetising.

Chilwars (small fish) prepared as before described, make a good dish for breakfast, and any other fresh-water fish which can be procured—*rooe* cut in thick slices and fried, spatchcocked eels, carp-roes, &c.

Omelets of various kinds—plain, *au jambon, aux rognons,* with fresh chillies, tomatoes, limes, and minced veal, chicken, or game can be made; only in using any such ingredients they should be chopped up very fine indeed.

Dumpoke is a good breakfast dish also. It is a boned chicken, stuffed with rice, chillies, and various ingredients, and served cold or hot.

Kegeree is another excellent dish. It is composed of the remains of cold fish; all the bones are extracted, and it is mixed with well boiled rice (about a cupful), two soft boiled eggs, salt and pepper to taste, half a teaspoonful of mustard, and one ounce of butter. These are all mixed together, made very hot, and served as quickly as possible.

Konftas are small round cakes made of the remains of any cold meat, minced and mixed with butter, yolk of egg, and spice; they are fried.

Spatchcock Fowl is a favourite dish with some people. I do not care for it, as the best part of the bird (the breast) is spoilt by its being split down, and so there never seems to be any meat on the chicken.

Kidneys filled with chopped parsley, well seasoned and buttered, are generally acceptable; also when stewed and served with mushrooms.

Potted meats of different kinds may make their appearance, and there should be cold meat on the side table, such as a spiced rump of beef, cold game, pies, tongue, &c.

Toasts, such as anchovy, ham, tongue, and chicken, remains of cold game and bacon, shrimps potted.

Grills of legs of duck, fowl, or game.

Bread, plain cakes, chupatees, and another sort of hot biscuit thicker than a chupatee, the name of which I forget, which a native cook usually sends in hot for breakfast; they are split and buttered in the same way that scones are at home.

Indian Corn (Zea Mays) is also eaten at breakfast. The green ears, when young, are roasted until brown, and sent to table with butter and salt. They are sometimes boiled instead of being roasted, the leaves taken off and served on toast with melted butter.

Fresh Fruit should always be on the table at this meal, for then it is more wholesome to eat than later on in the day. Melons are very much grown in India; the natives eat great quantities of them, as they are easy to cultivate. Bananas, the small sort, are not difficult to procure, are very cheap, and good eating. Dates, if you are in a date-palm (*Phœnix dactylifera*) country, are excellent, the fresh date being very wholesome. Sometimes, if the mornings are cool enough (this depends, of course, at what hour you breakfast), you can have your table spread in the verandah, with the blinds (chics) rolled up, just those in front of you, so that you can catch a peep of the trees and flowers in your compound, and, possibly a view of the surrounding country; it is more pleasant when tolerably cool than being in the house. This morning meal is one to dawdle over, for there are all the long hours of the day before you which you must perforce spend in the house, so "while the day is young," there is no occasion for hurry, and if friends drop in there is a certain amount of pleasant chatter going on which you do not care to curtail.

CHAPTER XIII.

SOCIETY.

Daily Duties—Social Customs and Observances—Calls—Visits—Tiffin—Agreeableness of Indian Society—Occupation and Health—Miseries of the Hot Season—Off to the Hills.

THE daily household duties to be performed by every lady are much the same in India as elsewhere. After breakfast the khánsámán has to be interviewed as before described, his previous day's bill looked over, checked, and paid, arrangements made for any extra things required, &c. Then will come a visit to the "go-downs" (store cupboards), which will most likely be in the verandah. From them you will give out all that is required for the day by the cook, the bearer, the khitmutgar, and the syces; the groceries for kitchen use, the oil for the lamps, corn (gram) for the horses, cows, or goats, if you keep them—for corn of all kinds should always be kept under lock and key, and given out daily as required, or else you will find it lasts but little time. This duty over, you will most likely see that your tailor (durzee) is supplied with the work you require him to do during the day. You will give a look round the different rooms to see that the proper amount of dusting has been done, and by that time you will be very glad to rest awhile, and read or write, until it is time for tiffin.

Luncheon in India is not held in much esteem, unless sometimes in the cold season, because, even when the weather is comparatively cool for most of the day, between twelve and one o'clock it is always too warm to sit down to a regular hot repast; hence "tiffin" is usually a meal of rather a light nature, at which cold meats and potted things, fruit, cheese, and cakes play the principal part. In the hot weather it is certainly rather superfluous to have a heavy meal at this hour, for the appetite has not had time to recover itself from breakfast, and as there is usually the five o'clock cup of tea, or else some iced liquid, which answers the purpose of tea at that time, and the dinner hour is tolerably early, say, half-past six or seven, so as to allow of a drive or ride in the cool of the evening, there is really no necessity for much more than quite light refreshments in the middle of the day. I am now writing of life in the plains. Besides, visiting very often interferes with the luncheon hour. It is an extraordinary fact that in India formal visits are paid just in the very hottest part of the day, but such is the case, and from twelve o'clock to two o'clock you will have to make your first visits. The fashion of calling is reversed from what it is in England. The people newly arrived in a station call on those who are resident in that station. Hence, when you have got tolerably settled in your new quarters, you will have to go the round of the station, calling first on the head military and civil residents.

In a very large station, such as Bombay, Calcutta, Lahore, &c., you could not call on everyone—that is, on all the married couples; but you would pay visits to the chief people, and then confine your calls more exclusively to your own more immediate set, such as the military people, if you are military, the civilians, if you are civilian. In all cases it is desirable to ascertain what people are visited, or you may, by inadvertently calling on every one, make things afterwards very awkward for yourselves. You must, therefore, be guided, to a certain extent, by what is the custom of the station with regard to paying visits and such matters of social etiquette, as in different places different customs are followed.

After your first calls have been returned, and as you become more intimate with the people whose acquaintance you wish to keep up, you can waive ceremony somewhat in the hours of calling, and do your visiting in the cool of the evening instead of the extreme heat of the day.

How I used to dread the round of formal visits! You arrived at the house in a parboiled state, for no covered conveyance can keep out the heat of these midday hours. If you were not told that "the door is shut" (*darwaza bund*) by the bearer who came to the door, you would probably be ushered into a room so dark —shaded to keep out the heat—that coming in from the glare of outside you would not for some time see anything distinctly, and find yourself addressing some undistinguishable mass of humanity, in reality the lady of the house. The awkwardness of these formal visits the new comer, however, soon ceases to regard; it is only at first that it seems a strange and uncomfortable mode of proceeding.

Unmarried men, of course, call on the married people, whether they are new comers or not. I remember how very indignant I felt on being told on one of my first visits by the bearer, *darwaza bund*. I did not then understand that it was only the Indian way of telling the society falsehood "not at home," which is so generally accepted in England, and scarcely felt inclined to be civil when that particular call was returned; but I made a mistake, not an unnatural one, and, as forewarned is forearmed, I mention it here for the benefit of others. As a rule, English people in India are most hospitable and agreeable to strangers—not half so stiff, indeed, as they very often are in their own country, nor yet so inclined to stand upon their dignity or treat their acquaintances with so much ceremony.

Indian society is most agreeable, especially in a good sized station, for there is always some party going on every day. Lawn tennis is now the great amusement for afternoon gatherings—in my time it was Badminton—and now you may, in a large station, play every day at some of the bungalows. It is scarcely a cool amusement for such a climate, but it is the fashion, and so every compound of any size boasts its lawn tennis ground. These parties are chiefly confined, however, to the cool season. In the hot weather, all who can get leave, and can afford to rush off to the hills, do so, and the plain stations are more or less deserted; but few people are left behind, and they shut themselves up all day long, only going out in the early morning and late at night, after dinner. It is then that Indian life is very nearly unbearable, supposing you to be of the unfortunate few left behind. There are no parties of any kind, for the simple reason that there are no people left to entertain or to be entertained. Then it is that the strain of the climate really begins to tell on even the strongest, the most energetic begin to flag, and need all their energy and all their strength of mind to keep them from giving up in despair. Hour after hour, day after day, the heat seems to increase; you get no rest at night, even though you may have your bed taken out into the compound and a sort of impromptu punkah rigged up over it; you wake up with a sense of suffocation; you are irritated beyond measure by trifles; you hate the frogs who croak to each other the livelong night; the insects of all kinds drive you to distraction, goading you into an almost desperate state; and then, perhaps, when the heat is positively unenduable, comes a storm of dust, or possibly a welcome rain, and the air clears, the atmosphere becomes more tolerable, and your worn-out energies revive somewhat.

In the plains during the hot season you *must* get early morning exercise, or you will not keep your health. You must lie by during the day and come out again with the bats in the evening, and either drive by moonlight or sit out in your compound. You must live temperately, avoid anything of a very stimulating nature, such as spirits or too much meat. A vegetable and fruit diet is the best during the hot weather. But above all things, you must avoid giving way to the feeling of lassitude which, however stirring a person you may be, will assuredly creep over you. Even while confined to your bungalow you should employ your mind, though your body may be comparatively still, or you will become wretched, moped, and miserable; and do not give way to sleep during the day, or you will never get rest at night.

Unfortunately, I was obliged to spend two hot seasons in the plains one after the other, so I know pretty well how hard the heat is to bear, and I firmly believe that the only way to keep one's health under such circumstances is not to give way to the climate too much, but keep the mind and body, to a certain extent, actively employed. When I say this I do not mean that you should run any risks from undue exertion, or go out at hours when it is not safe to do so, but simply that you should never be really idle. In employment you forget the miseries of the time being, and the day slips on towards night more quickly than you could have fancied.

CHAPTER XIV.

DINNER PARTIES.

Special Menus — Resources of Native Cooks — Dishes — Table Decoration — Attendance.

THE first dinner party you give will be to you rather an important event, and one, perhaps, about which you may be a little nervous, especially if there are among the invited guests any such as you happen to know are of a rather critical turn of mind.

As far as the *menu* goes consult your khánsámán; if he is a good one you need have little fear about the result of his share of the entertainment, and he will probably be able to give you a good deal of advice respecting the different dishes in season, all in a most respectful way. A dinner party is always an event of grave importance to your cook, his dignity is at stake, he feels that on him devolves a grave responsibility, and if your guests are those who hold an important position in the station, either military or civil "big wigs," he will rise to the occasion, and give you and your guests a far better dinner than many cooks would at home.

How the good dinners are cooked, which one partakes of in India, is a marvel, and I am always filled with astonishment at the way a good khánsámán will manage with, literally speaking, only a few pots and pans, for a set of dechsies such as he uses would fill an English cook with scorn. He has no *bain-Marie* to keep his sauces and gravies hot; no hot plate on which to stand his made dishes; no contrivances or aids to the culinary art; but yet the result shows him to be, in nine cases out of ten, a thorough master of cooking in all its branches, even to making rich wedding cakes, icing them over, and covering them with elegant ornaments. I remember on one occasion a young lady, who was engaged to an officer in India, came out to stay with us to be married from our house. She had brought her wedding cake with her, a very elaborate production, only, unfortunately, the icing and ornamental sugaring had all broken in the packing, though the cake itself was intact. My khánsámán, on observing our dismay when we unpacked it, hastened to assure me, in his native language, that he would set all that right again. This he certainly did, for on the eventful day the cake appeared beautifully ornamented with a representation of the Taj Mahal wonderfully well executed in white sugar; he had done it all himself, and the result could not have been better.

In arranging for a dinner party—*burra khana*, as your khánsámán will call it—you must give him timely notice. If you belong to a "mutton club," you will probably have arranged to get a saddle for your share that week, or a haunch, as the case may be. In a club of this sort the different members get the prime joints in turns, or else write their names against the joints they wish when the list is sent round by the manager. A well, that is "gram-fed," haunch or saddle of mutton is always appreciated in India, because it is by no means easy to get.

It is a mistaken idea that in India you should set before your guests as many English dishes as possible. The consequence is, you have tinned salmon, tinned peas, tinned ham, bottled fruits, and what are generally termed *Belatee* (English) stores given you at every dinner party until you are wearied at the sight of them, and loathe all tinned things for the rest of your life.

There is no reason why those Indian fruits, vegetables, fish, game, &c., which are in season, should not be used; only we all so much resemble a flock of sheep—we must do as our leader does; and as the fashion is to set as many English things as possible on the table, English people follow it *ad nauseam*.

In making out the following menus, I have given a good many Indian dishes—English dishes you can have, of course, if you prefer them—and as far as fish is concerned, you will have to fall back on tinned salmon very often, because there is nothing else to be had, unless you are in Bombay, where you can get pomplet, either white or black, the black being considered the better; mullets can sometimes be procured, also rooe, seer, chilwars (before mentioned), and mahsur, murrell. Game of various kinds is plentiful, the best being teal, sand grouse, quail, snipe, bustard, ortolans, partridges (black and grey), pheasants, plovers (green, grey, and golden), peahen, and florican, wild duck and wild goose. These are all to be had, but some are very insipid to the taste, partridges and pheasants especially. Venison, too, is easy to get, but it is quite unlike English venison, and not much esteemed. Vegetables of all kinds can be procured, and also fruits, but I cannot say very much for Indian fruit—the Cabul fruit is the best you can have.

Your dinner party is, I will suppose, for ten or twelve, including yourselves. Now that dining *à la Russe* is universal in India, as well as at home, it is no longer necessary to provide so many dishes as it used to be when they were placed on the table, and it was considered correct to match them; therefore there are not so many difficulties for a housekeeper to contend with. The table should be prettily decorated with flowers, arranged in any way that fancy dictates, only not in high glasses which hide the guests from each other; nothing is more absurd than to see two people seated at opposite sides of the table trying to look at each other by dodging first one side and then the other of a mass of obstructive greenery. Trails of ivy, ferns, and creepers, are now merely laid on the cloth, and either tiny low glasses of flowers placed in and out between them, or else long, low glass troughs are arranged down the centre and at the corners. The dessert should be tastefully set out, ornamented with leaves. In India there is no difficulty whatever about attendance, so the hostess need never trouble herself on that score; each guest brings his own servant to wait on him, and a married couple would bring with them two table servants. It is quite a pretty sight to see these natives all dressed in spotless white, relieved only by their coloured cummerbunds and badges in their turbans; they move about very noiselessly, and wait well, so that a *dîner à la Russe* in India is quite as well conducted an affair as in England, very often more so, as there are more attendants. A little instruction it will perhaps be necessary to give the khánsámán who carves at the side table, as to the helps he puts on the plates, and the way he cuts the joints, but he will soon get into the way of it. Servants have plenty of practice in large stations, for there are usually a good many dinner parties, and by going from house to house with you they soon become expert in such matters.

MENU I.

POTAGES.
Almond soup.   Clear gravy soup.

POISSONS.
Pomplet.   Tinned salmon.

ENTRÉES.
Croquettes of sweetbreads.   Beef olives with tomatoes.
Quenelles of partridge.

RELEVÉS.
Boiled turkey.   Haunch of mutton.

RÔTS.
Teal.   Quails.

ENTREMETS.
Maraschino jelly.   Burnt cream.
Meringuées filled with mango cream.

CHEESE.
Fresh.   Stilton.

ICES.
Lemon ice cream.   Coffee ice cream.

DESSERT.
Fruits in season.   Cakes, biscuits, &c.

The vegetables to serve with this menu would be as follows:

- Potatoes à la Maître d'Hotel.
- French beans à la Française.
- Green peas.
- Tomatoes with the beef olives.
- Cucumber with the salmon.

For the Indian dishes I give the recipes:

Almond Soup.—This is one of the best white soups, but it must be made very carefully. Stock from knuckles of veal and fat slices of ham, seasoned with sweet herbs and white pepper. Boil a fowl, take off all the meat, cut it into slices and pound in a marble mortar. Blanch 4oz. of almonds, pound these up very fine, and mix with the pounded fowl; add from six to eight tablespoonfuls of cream. If you cannot get cream and have to use milk instead, the yolks of two eggs must be added. Rub the whole through a sieve. Add about a tablespoonful of arrowroot to make the soup of the proper thickness; this should be mixed with a little stock before it is added to the whole. The soup must not be allowed to boil, and must be carefully stirred. If it boils it will curdle, which will spoil it. Its beauty is in its perfect smoothness.

Pomplet or Pomfret.—If procurable, this is generally fried in slices. The *entrées, relevés,* and *rôts* need no explanation; they would all be cooked as at home. The way to cook quails has already been stated in a former chapter. Teal are stuffed with crumbs of bread, chopped parsley, pepper, salt, nutmeg, and lime juice, mixed with the livers chopped very fine; they are sent to table on toast, and fresh green limes served with them; sometimes a sharp gravy is sent up also.

Maraschino Jelly.—Make the same as ordinary calf's foot jelly, only, of the maraschino, two liqueur glassfuls, besides two of brandy, should be added when the jelly is melted, before it is run through the bag.

Meringues.—Indian cooks make these very well, but insist on calling them "Mary Annes." Instead of filling them, when made, with whipped cream, fill them with rich mango fool or cream, to which some curaçoa should be added.

Burnt Cream.—Take a pint of cream, boil it with the peel of a lime, sweeten with pounded sugar, beat with the yolks of six eggs and the whites of four; add one tablespoonful of arrowroot, one of orange flower water, one dessertspoonful of ratafia. Strain the cream; when quite cold, add the other ingredients to it. Stir it over the fire until it is quite thick, put it into a dish, sprinkle sifted sugar over it, and brown with a salamander. It is eaten cold, sometimes iced.

Ices can, of course, only be given by those who possess a freezing machine, which is a luxury very few can boast of in India. Dr. Riddell says that Masters' is the best for the purpose. Full directions for use would be given with the machine. The charge for machine No. 2 consists of

    4lb. sulphate of soda (Glauber salts).
    2¼lb. sal ammoniac.
    2¼lb. saltpetre.
    10 pints water to each pail.

These ingredients must be all well pounded. If Glauber salts are difficult to obtain, then more saltpetre and sal ammoniac must be used in the same proportion as above. Glauber salts are used in England because they are cheap. The salts must be quite free from dirt and minutely pounded, and the water added to them in the machine last of all. The way to prepare cream or water ice in the common freezing pail is to place the mixture to be frozen in the freezer and close it; beat the ice up small with the due proportion of salt, put it into the tub, and insert the freezer, which should be rapidly turned round. The cream, as it sticks to the side, must be scraped down with an ice spoon until it is frozen; the more the cream is worked to the side the smoother and better flavoured it is. I have tasted very good ices in India, and have tried in the *menus* to mention those I remember as being especially nice.

Lemon Ice Cream.—Rasp two lemons on sugar, scraping off into the basin you mix in, in which is a pint of cream. Squeeze the lemons, and add the juice, sweetened with $\frac{1}{2}$lb. of pounded sugar; mix well, and freeze. This makes about one quart of ice.

Coffee Ice Cream.—Roast (freshly) 6oz. of the best coffee; put the berries into the oven on a tin for about five minutes. Take 1 pint of cream and $\frac{1}{2}$ pint of milk, boil together, and put them into a can; put the coffee taken from the oven into the boiling cream, cover the can over until the contents are cold, then strain; add 1oz. of arrowroot and $\frac{1}{2}$lb. of sugar, boil like custard, stirring one way to prevent curdling, and then freeze. This quantity makes about 1 quart of ice.

Vegetables and fruit I shall write of elsewhere. The vegetables named are English grown, I will suppose, in your own garden. If possible, have fresh English vegetables for your parties; they are much appreciated, and tinned peas when you can have fresh are a mistake, though all very well when the season is over for the fresh ones. We had English peas in our garden at Christmas, and so there is no difficulty in having a rotation of crops of them.

Here is a second menu for a dinner party :

MENU II.

POTAGES.

Artichoke soup.   Hare soup.

POISSON.

Mahseer (if procurable); if not, Salmon tinned (fresh).

ENTRÉES.

Croustades of quails.   Curried eggs.   Quenelles of chicken.

RELEVÉS.

Bustard.   Saddle of mutton.

Dinner Parties.

Rôts.

Snipe.   Pheasants.

Entremets.

Fruit jelly.   Cocoa-nut pudding.   Italian cream.

Cheese.

Fresh cream cheese.   Grated Parmesan.

Ices.

Pine-apple ice cream.   Strawberry ice cream.

Dessert.

Fruits in season, &c.

Vegetables to serve with this dinner:

> New potatoes (if in season, if not, potato balls).
> Stewed celery.
> Cauliflower.

Artichoke Soup.—Take a sheep's head and feet, and of it make a clear broth; if a sheep's head is not procurable, a cold roasted fowl will do instead. Wash and cut up into slices these vegetables: two carrots, two turnips, two leeks, two onions, one head of celery—some cloves should be stuck in the onions; put all into a stewpan with the *consommé*; simmer the whole very gently for two hours, skimming off the fat as it rises. Wash and peel 2lb. of Jerusalem artichokes, put them into another stewpan with a little of the broth, boil until they are quite tender and can be rubbed through a coarse cloth or a hair sieve; strain the broth that remains, and add the artichokes with salt to taste; put all the stock back into the stewpan, skimming it carefully; mix a pint of cream with the yolks of two eggs well beaten, boil this, and add it to the stock. Serve with toasted bread cut into very small dice. A little fresh lime juice from green limes is a great improvement to this soup, only too much would spoil the flavour.

Mahseer.—This fish is styled the Indian salmon, but it really belongs to the barbels or carp. Mahseer are very fair eating, being good curried or kippered, or plain dressed, fried, or baked; they run to a very large size, from 20lb. to 60lb., and give very fair sport, taking a fly, but are more amenable to ground bait; a spoon is very killing, and the largest fish are caught by trolling. If you are near a river or a lake, you will be able to get various kinds of fresh-water fish; but I hardly ever remember eating anything but tinned salmon at a dinner party. We often had *mutchlee* (fish) of various kinds, and very good some of them were; during the breeding season, however, they are, of course, unfit to touch.

The *entrées* are made in the same way as usual. See any good cookery book.

Bustard.—These are very fine birds, and excellent eating; they weigh from 20 to 30lb. The bird is cleaned, trussed, and roasted in precisely the same way as a turkey; bread sauce is sent to table with it.

Snipe are very plentiful in some parts of India, and *pheasants* also. They are both dressed in exactly the same way they would be at home.

Fruit Jelly.—Ordinary calves' feet jelly, flavoured with wine and whole fruits, such as strawberries or greengages, put into the jelly just as it is about to set.

Cocoanut Pudding.—Grated cocoanut to the amount of $\frac{1}{4}$lb., $\frac{1}{4}$lb. of sugar, $3\frac{1}{2}$lb. of good butter, the whites of four eggs, half a glassful of sherry or brandy, and a teaspoonful of orange water. Line a pie dish with puff paste, pour in the mixture, and bake in a cool oven for about three-quarters of an hour; serve hot.

Italian Cream.—Rub on sugar the rind of three small fresh green limes, scrape off into a deep dish, add half a wineglassful of brandy, the juice of the limes, $2\frac{1}{2}$oz. of finely sifted sugar, and 1 pint of thick cream; work the whole up well with a whisk. Have ready 1oz. of isinglass, which should be boiled in a quarter of a pint of water until quite dissolved, strain it into the dish, beat it well, then fill a mould with it. When thoroughly set, turn out on to a glass dish, and garnish with candied lemon peel.

Pine Apple Ice Cream.—Pound a raw pine apple with sugar, add sugar and lemon juice to taste, 1 pint of cream, and a little new milk; mix well together; freeze. This makes about a quart, reckoning the pine apple at $\frac{1}{2}$lb. It can be made also with preserved pine apple, but is not so nice as when made with the fresh fruit.

Strawberry Ice Cream.—Made with fresh strawberries if they can be got, if not with strawberry jam, 1lb., the juice of two lemons, one pint of cream, a little new milk and sugar to taste; freeze. About one quart.

The following is a menu for a smaller party, and is more Indian in its character than those preceding:

MENU III.

POTAGE.
Mulligatawney soup.

POISSON.
Baked murrell.

ENTRÉES.
Pilau.   Fowl khubab.

RELEVÉ.
Haunch of black buck.

RÔT.
Sand grouse.

ENTREMETS.
Orange jelly.   Plantain pudding.
Indian ramakin.

CHEESE.
Fresh cream cheese.   Salad.

DESSERT.
Indian fruits only.

Vegetables served with this dinner:

Yams, brinjals, lal sag (sort of spinach).

Mulligatawney Soup.—Slice four or five onions very thin, put them, with four cloves of garlic and ¼lb. of butter, into a stewpan. Take a fowl or a rabbit, and divide as if for fricassee; season with white pepper. Put the meat—some people put a little beef and mutton besides the chicken—into the stewpan on the onions, cover the pan, and simmer the contents for half an hour. Prepare beforehand a paste made of the following ingredients:

Salt	1 Tolah.
Black pepper	1 Tolah.
Turmeric	1 Tolah.
Coriander seeds	4 Tolahs.
Fenugreek	½ Tolah.
Cayenne	1 Massa.

Kodianum leaves (4) to be added while boiling.

All these ingredients, except the leaves, must be well pounded in a mortar, and, when quite fine, mixed into a paste with a little clear gravy. Then add the paste and two quarts of clear gravy to the contents of the stewpan, and allow the whole to simmer gently for half an hour, add (about five minutes before taking off the fire) the juice of a lime and a little arrowroot. The kodianum leaves are also known as curry pak leaves.

A more simple way.—Cut up a good sized fowl into slices, put the meat into a stewpan with 2 quarts of water, some allspice and black pepper, and salt to taste. When it boils, skim carefully; let it simmer for one hour and a half, then strain. Put some bits of the meat into a stewpan, and fry them brown in butter, with three or four sliced onions. When quite done add the broth, put again on the fire, skim, and allow to simmer for half an hour; then mix two spoonfuls of curry powder and a little arrowroot with a teaspoonful of salt, and enough stock to thicken the soup. Let it simmer again until the meat is quite tender, add the juice of a green lime, and serve. Boiled rice is always sent to table with this soup.

Baked Murrell.—Stuff the fish with suet, bread crumbs, parsley, lime peel, and eggs, dredge it well with flour, and lay it in a deep dish. Pour in, on one side, a teacupful of rich gravy, in which has been mixed a lump of fresh butter, a tablespoonful of vinegar, pepper and salt. Put into a rather hot oven, and while the fish is baking baste continually with gravy.

Pilau.—Cut two ripe mangoes into very thin slices, peel and chop four large onions, and put them, with the mangoes, into a saucepan, with 4oz. of butter; have ready some squares of beef or mutton—they should have been fried in butter—put them into the stewpan on the top of the other ingredients, and stew the whole for one hour. Have also ready some well boiled rice, put it in the bottom of a deep dish, arrange the meat on the top, pour the gravy over it, and serve very hot.

Fowl Khubab.—Choose a plump young fowl, prick it well all over with a fork, rub it thoroughly with a paste composed of 1 chittack of coriander seed, ground up with 2 chittacks of green ginger, 2 mashas of cloves, 2 mashas of cardamoms, 2 mashas of salt, and 1 masha of black pepper. Fry four large onions, thinly sliced, with 6 mashas of turmeric pounded with 1 chittack of butter, adding to this 2 chittacks of cream. Roast the fowl and baste with the above mixture frequently. Serve very hot, and send some of the mixture to table as sauce to be eaten with it.

Haunch of Black Buck.—Black buck is rather despised, but it is, when good, excellent eating. It should be dressed in the usual way venison is done, and good gravy and currant jelly sent to table with it. The great secret of cooking any venison well is constant basting.

Sand Grouse.—Dressed as ordinary grouse.

Orange Jelly.—Scrape on sugar six limes, two Seville, and two sweet oranges, mix with the juice of the fruit, and let it stand for twelve hours. Boil $\frac{1}{2}$lb. of sugar in two wine-glasses of water; put it into a basin, and when it has cooled strain the juice into it. Dissolve 1oz. of isinglass in a pint of water, simmer until it is a strong jelly, then mix in the lemon juice and sugar; stir it until it is nearly cold, and then pour into a mould.

Plantain Pudding.—Fry some plantains in their skins; when done, peel them and cut into slices, add sugar to taste, the juice of three limes, the peel of one shred into tiny pieces, one glass of sherry, a few cloves, and a little butter. This is put into a paste and boiled as an apple pudding would be. Cream and sifted sugar are sent to table with it.

Indian Ramakins.—Take equal quantities of grated cheese, flour, butter, and one egg to each spoonful of the other ingredients, cayenne pepper and salt to taste; mix all thoroughly well together, and bake in ramakin cases. Serve very hot, and send made mustard to table with them.

Cheese.—The only cheese met with in India that is made in the country is cream cheese and fresh curd. English cheeses are imported, but are expensive to buy. Some of the fresh cream cheeses are very nice, but they will not keep long, and are usually eaten a few days after they are made.

This dinner would be too Indian to suit many people's taste, but I merely give it as an example. There are a great many excellent Indian dishes which people effect to despise, but very many of them are very good indeed. There is, however, in general too much ghee used; this should not be allowed, but butter be employed instead. With all your dislike to ghee it is used very often by your khánsámán, and you are charged for butter, which is more expensive.

CHAPTER XV.

GARDENING.

Irrigation—the Well—Water-drawing by Bullocks—the Indian Gardener — Hedging — Grass Plots — Manures — Native Deficiency in Agriculture—Melons—Beans—Peas—Cabbages —Asparagus — Onions — Mushrooms — Cucumbers — Cress —Luttuces — Endive — Tomatoes—the Egg Plant — Artichokes — Parsley—Carrots — Parsnips—Potatoes—Turnips — Pumpkins — Vegetable Marrow — Celery — Beetroot — Scorzonera—Spinach—Herbs—Yams—Maize, &c.

Most Indian houses have a plot of ground surrounding them. Ours stood in rather a larger compound than is usual, and we had, moreover, a very good supply of water, our well being a deep one, and in thorough repair.

Water is, in India, the one great requisite for a garden; with sufficient irrigation even the most arid, unpromising bit of ground, which at first sight appears incapable of growing anything, will yield good crops of vegetables, Indian corn (*zea mays*), melons, and nearly anything you like to grow on it. Even in the most barren compound, which is merely a sandy desert to look at, there is generally, if the bungalow standing in it is occupied, a small green spot outside the bath-room (*guslkhàna*), where the water runs out which is emptied from the baths, and coarse grass and common prickly-leaved shrubs spring up on the spot so watered.

In a former chapter, on choosing bungalows, I laid particular stress on the necessity of having a deep, properly built, and plentifully supplied well in the compound, even if the garden were not kept up, doubly necessary would it be to select a compound having this convenience if the ground is intended to be cultivated. It is scarcely possible to overrate the relief to the eye which is afforded by even a little greenery around the bungalow, and, when it can be made useful as well as restful and ornamental, it is certainly worth while to have a garden.

We had a large, but at first sight, apparently barren compound; it had a few nice trees in it, certainly, but it was open to the road, and was only a large patch of dusty, sandy ground, without a scrap of vegetation beyond the prickly shrubs which struggle up everywhere, even without any water. However, we soon altered this state of things by setting the well to work.

I had better describe the well. It was one of those in common use throughout India, like the Persian wells of world-old form, and of a very primitive kind. Surrounded by a deep shaft, lined with brickwork, was a wooden wheel revolving on a pivot. This, being turned by a bullock, which was blindfold, as it continually plodded in a circle, served to raise a succession of earthenware pots filled with water. Each pot turned over as it reached the head of the wheel, poured out its contents into a wooden trough, and then disappeared into the depths below to bring up a fresh supply. Of these pots there were a great number, and though the amount of water each brought up was not large, yet the combined contents, when the wheel was continued many hours at work, produced a considerable volume of water, which was guided by the trough into a shallow watercourse, running the entire length of our compound or grounds. This is the general method; and from the centre channel are cut little ditches, which lead round all the beds and plots of ground under cultivation. Each bed can, therefore, be flooded at will, and when it has been sufficiently irrigated the supply of water is drained off by a trench, and turned off into another channel, by which a fresh plot of ground is submerged in turn.

We bought a pair of bullocks very cheaply (for 10 rupees each, if I remember aright). They were, however, mere skin and bone, but soon got fat and fit for work under good food and careful treatment. Our well, too, was going all day, and until quite late at night, one bullock on and then the other, in turns. Good bullocks, of course, cost much more than this, from 30 to 50 rupees the pair.

The gardener (*mallee*) is a very important person. The Indian mallees are, according to their lights, very intelligent, hard-working men; they follow in the steps of those who have gone before, and abhor all new-fashioned ways, thinking that as things went on years ago, so they must continue to go. If their ideas are primitive, their implements are even more so. A garden knife and the very rudest of spades suffice a mallee for every sort of work in his domain. Squatting down on his heels, he digs away with the former all day, and if given English tools, declines to use them. The first task ours undertook was to grow hedges all round the compound, in order to shut it out from the road and screen us from the gaze of the passers-by, and this is how he set about it. With the assistance of the garden coolie, by name Laloo, he dug a trench round the place, which was about two and a half acres in extent, and then other trenches to mark the entrances, of which there were two in front of the house and two at the back. The trenches were then thickly sown with a very quick growing privet, called by the natives *gyte*. So rapidly does this shrub develop that one can almost see the advances it makes each day. The trenches being flooded with water for several hours morning and evening, the gyte grew in a wonderfully short time into a thick close hedge; from just appearing above the top of the trench it soon advanced to the height of 4ft. or 5ft., at which it was kept cut. I think the botanical name of this privet is *Lawsonia alba;* anyhow, it made an excellent screen, and was very refreshing to the eye. We also divided off a croquet ground with it. To make this ground we had to plant it with grass—an operation performed in a most primitive manner by the native mallees. They do not sow grass seed, nor yet plant out sods of turf, as would be done at home, but simply chop up cut grass, and either dibble it in, or mix it up with *muttee* (mud), and plaster it on the ground, which is afterwards kept under water constantly until the grass begins to grow, which—when once it has made a fair start— it does very rapidly. We had two grass plots—one in front of the house and one at the back—where the goats were usually tethered.

The produce of your compound depends, of course, somewhat on the nature of the soil, but even if that is not very good, it can, by constant irrigation and manuring, be very much improved. Keeping horses, bullocks, goats, and rabbits, there should be no difficulty, with care, in having the soil of your compound enriched, if it is naturally poor; only you must look after such matters yourself, or your native servants will use the manure as fuel. Care should be taken of all sweepings from stables, bullock houses, &c., and also of bones, garden rubbish, vegetable matter, &c., all of which should be collected in heaps.

Liquid manure is also required, and can easily be made by adding to a gallon of water ½oz. of sulphate of ammonia. Only it must not be had recourse to too often; for plants in pots it is excellent, but they must be watered with plain water at least four times before the dose is repeated.

The natives are slow to learn the value of manures, allowing refuse vegetable matter to waste instead of using it on the land, and using manure for fuel. This they are now almost obliged to do—that is, in those parts where wood is not available for the purpose—but it is a proceeding which it is to be hoped the new Director of Agriculture will endeavour to check, for the evils arising from it are very great. The soil is rapidly, under this system of spoliation, becoming less fertile, for it stands to reason that, by such a method, all is taken from the ground by degrees, and little or nothing restored. If manure from cattle is not available, then artificial manures should be used instead, and every care taken and use made of vegetable refuse, bones, the mud from ponds and small pieces of water, and so on.

It is not the small farmer or ryot who is at fault in his agricultural knowledge, for it is wonderful how much he really knows about farming—that is, after a primitive fashion—but the fact that wood ashes and manure from cattle are the soil enrichers he has been accustomed to use, as his fathers did before him, and if they are not procurable he will not seek for others, but fold his hands and whisper "kismet," while his land becomes poorer and poorer each year, and the crops he gets off it smaller and smaller.

But by gradual and careful teaching and practical supervision, the ryot may be taught much, and it is just this which the recently revised agricultural department has in its power to do, if it is well carried out, and if high farming is not too much insisted on.

Melons are a favourite food in India, especially with natives, and grow very well in most parts; we had about a quarter of an acre planted with them, not confining ourselves to one kind, but growing green, pink, and yellow-fleshed as well. Cut fresh for breakfast, they are an excellent and very wholesome fruit, especially tempting when iced on a very hot day. A good *khurbooza*, as the natives call a melon, is a food by no means to be despised. The rock, green, and musk melons all grow well in light sandy soils, and are sown at the same time. It is usual to sow the seed in November; three or four seeds are planted together, the ground having been previously manured. The plants must not be allowed, as they come up, to remain too close together, but be weeded out, leaving a distance of from 5ft. to 7ft. between each. They are ready to cut about March, and continue bearing for three months or more. The turbooza, or water melon (so called to distinguish it from the other kinds), is in season about the same time. We always saved the seeds of those melons we fancied had a more than usually good flavour, and sowed them when the proper time came round. I brought home a quantity of seed, and found the sorts answered very well at home when grown in a hotbed. The green melon has, perhaps, the richest flavour, but many of the others are very good, some water melons in particular being of especially pleasant taste.

We brought out a great variety of vegetable seeds with us—beans, peas, &c. The peas did very well. English peas are considered a delicacy, but the country peas are very nice, and there are many varieties. *Buttana* is the Hindostani name for this vegetable. The commonest peas in the country are the brown, large white, and green; the common pigeon pea (*Cajanus Indicus*) is much liked and very largely used by the natives, who rank it very highly as a cheap and nutritious food, and eat it mixed with rice. June is the usual month in which to commence sowing ordinary peas, and it is easy to have a succession of crops, sowing continually from June to February. They should be sown in double rows, not too deep—about 2in.—and a good space left between each row. When they are commencing to climb, the rows should be well earthed up on each side, room being left for the water to run in the centre, and stout sticks should be placed in the space in the middle of the rows; freedom from weeds, good manuring, and irrigation when necessary, constitute the treatment under which they generally thrive. Weak, poor-looking plants should be weeded out, and the strongest saved for seed. If you do not stick them, they must be grown over piles of brushwood, similarly to tomatoes.

Beans, country sorts as well as English, are sown in the same way as peas—in drills. Each bean should be dibbled in about 6in. apart from its neighbour; they should be sown in November, and later if a succession of crops is wanted. Any light soil does for them, with a little manuring and care in weeding, irrigation, &c. The seed should be changed every season, as it very soon deteriorates—much sooner than pea seed. This applies to the broad and Windsor kinds. French beans grow well, both dwarf and runners; they are sown from October till March, or, indeed, up to June; but caterpillars prove very destructive to them, as also does the *Mylabris cichorea*, a fly which feeds on the flower. These beans must not be planted too close, and they should be well sticked when they commence climbing.

Cabbages of various sorts can be grown with success, *Kobee*, the ordinary cabbage, cauliflower (*Phool kobee*), borecole (*Phultee kobee*), which grows splendidly—the sprouts are, of course, the only parts fit to eat—and many other kinds. Seed for most sorts should be sown in May, and the plants must, from the time they begin to show, be carefully watched for caterpillars, which are terribly destructive to cabbages, and should be destroyed at once. A good plan is to sprinkle the young plants, after they have been watered, with a little black pepper or pounded turmeric. Either will keep the caterpillars off, or cause them to quit the leaves; plants so treated will also be avoided by slugs. Some people sow cabbage seed first of all in boxes, transplant to other boxes when grown about an inch high, and when the young plants are pretty strong, finally set out in the beds where they are to remain. The soil should be rich, but not heavy, for all the cabbage tribe.

Asparagus, called by the natives *Marjhooba Nokdoon*, we cultivated largely. There are two methods of growing it. One is by sowing the seed broadcast in beds about 6ft. square, and then, when the plants are about 8in. high, transplanting them into trenches, having between each trench a space of 12in. The roots must be well covered, and the soil in the trenches must be rich, good manure being dug into it. The other method is to sow the seed in long beds about 20in. wide, where the plants are to remain; this is the least trouble, and answers very well if the soil is prepared and enriched and the beds are kept well watered; but they cannot, of course, be worked for some time. When the first lot of plants has gone to seed, the beds must no longer be watered, but the stalks allowed to wither; their roots should be very carefully uncovered, so that the crowns are not injured, and re-covered with old manure of a rich character to the depth of 2in., turning over on to it the spare soil left between the rows; this will form a watercourse between the trenches, and the roots below will thus get their fair share of moisture. It is usual to irrigate daily, or at least every second day, as it causes the plants to send up a more plentiful supply of shoots. As the latter get thin, the beds should no longer be cut from, but the asparagus allowed to run to seed, and then the roots manured again as the stalks wither off. Well-grown asparagus is much appreciated in India. It is even iced and handed as an *entremet* at large dinners, but I cannot say, beyond the fact of its being a novelty, that it is at all improved by the process. Our *mallee* was particularly successful in growing it; he treated it by the second method described, allowing it to mature in the same bed in which it was first sown.

Onions, called in Hindustani *peeaz*, are easily grown all over India, and are much used there, as with us, in cooking. The usual way of cultivating them is to sow broadcast and prick out into beds when strong enough, leaving about 10in. between each plant. They are sown all the year round, and are very easy to grow.

Mushrooms (*Koodrattee*) are, after the rainy season and during its continuance, found in most places; they are just the same as those indigenous to this country, and the good and wholesome sorts are distinguished from the bad and poisonous by precisely the same signs—their pink colour, deepening in tint as they get old; their peculiar smell, and the readiness with which the skin will peal off. They are a nice addition to many dishes. Quails taste very good stuffed with them instead of green chillies. They are served in the same ways as at home—on toast, as an *entrée* with claret sauce and a dash of green lime juice, and pickled.

Cucumbers (*kheera*) are easily grown all over India, the natives being very partial to them. They are allowed to grow very much *au naturel*, creeping over sticks or trellis-work as they please, only not planted too close together. The fruit is not so fine, certainly, as that grown in England in hotbeds, but, though much smaller, the flavour is quite as good, if not better, and there is no difficulty about cultivating them; they do not require so much water as many other crops, and can be sown and matured at all seasons.

Their greatest enemies are porcupines and jackals; this is why they are grown on lattice work, or over high sticks, as they are then out of the reach of such vermin.

Cress (*hallam*).—It is considered quite an amusement to grow cress in boxes. If sown thick in narrow drills and well watered, it can be grown all the year round in the garden. Watercress also can, with a little management, be easily cultivated. A series of shallow beds at different levels, so that as one bed is full of water it overflows into the one below it, is a good plan to adopt, for this answers the purpose of running water. If the water runs off the lowest bed into a channel, which returns to the main channel, the water can be kept running while the well is working without much waste, as in the short time that the well is stopped the beds, though they may possibly drain out, will take no hurt. Some people grow cress in barrels in the same way, always letting the water be moving, not stagnant.

Lettuces of various sorts can be grown the whole year through. A great business of ours used to be to go round in the mornings and tie up the lettuces to give them good hearts. They should be sown first of all in very small beds, then pricked out into larger ones, and 12in. allowed between each lettuce. After being transplanted they give little trouble. The soil for them should be light, but rich.

Endive.—Either the curled or the flat-leaved kind is sown in beds or boxes, and pricked out when about 2in. high into those in which it is to remain. From 10in. to 12in. should be allowed between each plant, and when they have reached their proper growth they must be tied up to bleach—if they are bleached in the same way as often practised at home, that is, a board placed on them, the white ants will soon find them out, so tying up is the safest plan to pursue.

Tomatoes (Belatee Begun) grow splendidly in India, though they are not indigenous to the country, but are natives, I believe, of South America. The single and double sorts flourish equally well. The way our *mallee* treated them was to sow them in small plots of ground first of all, and then transplant out in rows and set the plants some distance apart—about 22in.—having a space of fully 2ft., if not more, between the rows. They are staked with strong sticks, or else piles of brushwood are laid between the rows, leaving the watercourses clear, and they are allowed to climb over them; this was how we grew them, and when we came home I got our old gardener to adopt the same plan. They seem to ripen better, as they can be turned round and propped so that the underneath side, which too often in this climate does not ripen properly, gets the sun also. If sown in India in June, they will be ripe in October, and the crops can be kept up from then to April.

Egg Plant (Solanum Melongena), called by the natives *Brinjal* or *Binegun*, is much used in India. It grows very easily, and there are several varieties, one of which has a round purple or white fruit; another a longer and much more oval-shaped fruit, white or red; and another striped red. They are propagated by seed, which is sown just before the rainy season; the plants are moved when strong enough to where they are to remain. Brinjals are plainly dressed as vegetable marrows are, and served on toast with butter, or they are curried or roasted, and fried in butter and *dhall;* in any way they are very good.

Artichokes (Kungur).— Two only are cultivated for use out of the four species that there are; these are the French and the Dutch. The seed for either kind is usually sown in June, and the sowing continued during the rains; it is planted some inches—from 6in. to 8in.—apart. When the artichokes have put out six leaves they must be transplanted in rows about 3ft. apart; the ground into which they are put should have been previously well dressed. They will have to be looked at very frequently for "black fly," as, if this pest is not destroyed, all the leaves will be eaten up. The best remedy is to dust charcoal ashes thickly over the leaves, or else water them overhead with tobacco-water, poured on with a very fine rosed watering-pot. English seed grows well in India, also that from the Cape. Only one head should be allowed, of the globular kind, to remain on each stalk; all the others must be picked off; the one left will then become very fine. They are dressed in precisely the same way, when eaten plain, as they would be in this country, but the natives prepare them in other ways very well. They serve them cold as an *entremet,* with butter, anchovy, beetroot, capers, pickled cucumbers, and pour over all a rich salad sauce, garnishing with cress, parsley, slices of hard-boiled eggs, &c.; fried in quarters they are especially good, and this way of cooking them might easily be adopted in England. They must be quite young and tender, quartered, then pared, and rubbed over with lime or lemon to keep the colour and prevent their turning black; the leaves are nearly all trimmed off, leaving, of course, the edible ends; the quarters are then washed and drained on a sieve, next put with pepper, salt, and the juice of a green lime, or, in default of that, lemon juice, into a dish; three eggs are then beaten up in a teaspoonful of olive oil and three tablespoonfuls of flour; the artichokes are put into the mixture and stirred round with a wooden spoon until they are well covered with the sauce, then fried in dripping, the quarters being put in one at a time, drained on paper or a clean cloth, and served with a garnish of either fresh green parsley or else fried parsley. These recipes apply to the Dutch kind. Jerusalem artichokes are also cooked in the ways adopted with us, boiled, stewed in thick white sauce, and fried with a slice or two of onion, minced parsley, vinegar, salt, and pepper. They are best, I think, in soup, a recipe for which I have already given in a former chapter.

Parsley (Ajmood) is, of course, grown in every garden; it is sown where it is to remain, in rows or beds, thinned out, and well watered. English seed should always be used, it is so very much better than the common parsley of the country. Carefully treated, it will last all the year round, only the leaves should be cut down quite close to the roots sometimes, as the plants then throw up fresh young shoots.

Carrots, called in Hindustani *Gajur*, grow freely everywhere, as they are indigenous to India; the red and yellow are the two kinds cultivated. They are sown broadcast where they are to remain, and thinned out as they require it; a space of at least 6in. should be left between the roots. We grew a quantity, giving them to the horses as a treat every now and then. By cutting off the green tops in April they will keep until July, as their growth is thereby checked. Soil for them should be light, but good.

Parsnips (juzur) are much more difficult to grow; the seeds very rarely come up properly, to begin with. The seed should be sown in July, and the roots are fit to eat in March or April. We tried them for a time, but, finding they were troublesome and not at all good, we gave up their cultivation. Possibly the soil did not suit them.

Potatoes I should certainly have mentioned before; the *aloo* is a very important vegetable, and can, in some parts of India, be grown the whole year round—that is, on the hills. White ants are the great enemies of the potato, and as light and loamy a soil as possible should therefore be chosen to grow them in. They are planted usually in rows about a foot apart, and should be set 6in. deep in the ground. Before the rains is the best time to put them in; water should never be allowed to lodge around them, so they should not be watered too much. The slices (each slice should have two well developed eyes) must be dipped while fresh cut in wood ashes, the cut side being the side to dip. Let them dry, which they will do in a few hours, and then plant. This treatment, the *mallees* say, keeps off the ants' attacks. Grubs also eat this vegetable, and are most destructive to it. Very fine potato crops are yielded in some parts of the Deccan;

there they sow from October to December. The plants must be searched for the caterpillar grub constantly; the grubs are, it is now ascertained, the larvæ of the black beetle, the eggs being in the manure with which the ground is dressed before the potatoes are set. No effectual remedy has as yet been found for this plague, beyond the simple one of searching for them daily and destroying them when found. Lately much more attention has been paid to the cultivation of this vegetable in India, and with very good results.

The natives dress the *aloo* in much the same way we do at home. I do not remember tasting it prepared in any especially Indian fashion.

Turnips (*Shalgam*) are easily cultivated in most parts of India; in the Deccan they flourish well. They are usually sown at the commencement of the rainy season, and they continue until the end of February, sometimes into March. European seed is always used. The soil must be light, but rich; it is usual to sow broadcast, and then transplant either in ridges or rows, leaving about 12in. between each plant. Search the plants carefully for caterpillars, as the leaves, especially during the rains, are infested with them, and if they are not picked off they will completely destroy them. Swede and Cashmere turnips should be sown in July, Globe in August, large Globe and Herefordshire in September.

Pumpkins (in Hindustani *Kuddoo*) grow very well, requiring but little care. They are sown usually when the rains commence, in a light, but good soil. They are often cooked when quite young, and not much larger than a hen's egg, and should be sliced and gently boiled, and served with melted butter with a dash of lime juice in it. They also make good soup when young; they are stewed for this until tender in white stock, then pressed through a sieve, and half a pint of cream added before the soup is served; the cream must be heated, and pepper and salt to taste added.

Vegetable Marrows (called by the natives *Suppra roomro*) are propagated only by seed; the pear-shaped kind are the best to grow, but they must be eaten when quite young, or they get stringy. These vegetables should be sown where they are to remain in March and April, as they do not bear transplanting well. They are dressed in the same ways as at home, plain boiled when quite young, and served on toast with melted butter; also made into soup in the same way as pumpkins.

Celery (Ujoodeen).—The seed should be sown as the rains commence, in boxes first of all, and then the young plants pricked off into fresh boxes, and, finally, when about five weeks old, moved into the trenches where they are to remain. The trenches are thus prepared: Dig out earth to the depth of 1½ft. by 2ft. wide, laying the earth level between the trenches, which should be 4ft. apart. Into each trench put 1ft. good manure, and over this 6in. of the earth that was dug out. Mix the earth and manure well up together and smooth off the surface. When this has been done, the earth at the side of each trench will be 6in. or 8in. higher than the surface of the trench. Place the young plants in double rows 10in. apart every way; in about a fortnight a little earth should be drawn up around the necks of the plants, only be careful that no earth gets into the hearts of them. This operation should be repeated every ten days until the celery is as large as you wish; earth up when the plants are dry. Water freely every day, if necessary. Transplant offshoots so as to have a succession of plants coming on all the year round.

Celery is excellent stewed in veal stock until quite tender, and then, before serving, strain on it a quarter of a pint of cream, the well-beaten yolks of two eggs, some lime juice, grated nutmeg, salt and pepper to taste, and a very little butter; this sauce should be well mixed, and made hot before being strained on to the celery. This recipe is for a white stew; if it is wished brown, it must be stewed in a good brown gravy instead of white stock, and the cream and eggs omitted; season with pepper, salt, and mace.

Celery seed should always be saved, as it is most useful for flavouring soups, sauces, &c.

Beetroot, both red and white, can be easily grown. The seed should be sown from May to September, or even later if a succession is wanted. Sow in small beds and transplant, when ready, to rows; plant at least 12in. apart. Procure fresh seed each year, and remember the soil can hardly be too light. Beetroot (or *chukunda*) is dressed as in England, baked, stewed, or plain boiled, sliced and eaten cold with vinegar, also pickled.

Scorzonera is an annual introduced from Europe. Salsify is the black scorzonera; both are treated in the same way—sown broadcast in small beds, and then pricked out into larger ones. They grow freely after the rains. As vegetables, they make an agreeable change, dressed as they are here, and sometimes with cheese, which is grated and sprinkled over the scorzonera or salsify when it is cooked, then put in the oven to bake, and browned over with a salamander before serving.

Spinach (*palung*) should be sown in the rains, July to September, according to place, in lines 1ft. apart. It requires to be watered, not too much; dressed as at home.

Herbs are largely grown.

Basil, Sweet Borage (*Boomak Kalee Toolsee*) is grown as a shrub in all parts of India; it is, if sown, put in in August and September.

Marjoram, which is a native of India, is sown at the same time as basil; it is easily reared by seed, roots, or slips, and is much used in flavouring.

Mint, known as *Podeena*, of which there are three sorts—spearmint, peppermint, and pennyroyal—is propagated by layers, or parting the roots or cuttings. It is very largely grown; the first named is the kind used in cooking. All sorts are subject to a tiny black caterpillar, which eats the leaves and will destroy very quickly a whole bed if the precaution is not taken of flooding it.

Fennel grows very freely all over India; it dies down directly the seed has ripened, being an annual. It is generally sown in rows, but needs very little attention.

Sage grows, too, very easily; it is not, however, a native of India, but was introduced from Europe; it can be propagated from cuttings, layers, or roots with equal ease. It is a perennial.

Thyme, on the contrary, is by no means an easy plant to rear, and is best raised from seed and grown in pots. It requires a very good soil.

Garlic is common all over the country, the natives call it *lussun*, and grow it freely in their gardens, as they use it very much in cooking their food—mixing it with rice, fish, &c. It is best grown from the root; a bulb is broken, the cloves extracted, and planted in beds from 4in. to 6in. apart. It needs but little care, only when the leaves dry and wither, the roots should be taken up and preserved in a dry place.

Mustard is cultivated a good deal, both the white and the black kinds, the former for salad, the latter for pickles, sauces, and oil; it is called by the natives *Rai*, and is cultivated in the same way as cress; it is sown at the same time in July and August, at intervals of ten days, so as to keep up the supply for salads.

Chives are propagated easily by slips or else dividing the roots; 10in. should be allowed between each clump.

Shallots are grown in the same way, the chive being a species of shallot.

Horse Radish is not cultivated in India, but there is a substitute for it, the root of the mooringa, a tree which is indigenous to the country. The roots are scraped and used instead of horse-radish, and have the same properties and much the same flavour. It is easily propagated by seed.

Capsicums, called *Buragach Mirchee*, are known all over India, the red pepper obtained from them being so much used in cooking. They require little care, for they grow anywhere well, provided the ground is enriched with a little manure, The seed is sown first of all broadcast, and the young plants pricked out into rows, leaving a distance of $1\frac{1}{2}$ft. between each plant. They require a good deal of water, and must be kept free from weeds. This plant is a native of South America, and there are many varieties of it, which are distinguished by the shape of the fruit. Cayenne pepper is the produce of the smaller species of capsicum; the fruits are dried, pounded, and mixed with salt. When gathered and eaten fresh they are very wholesome, and good promoters of digestion in tropical countries. Green chillies are much used in native curries, in dishes prepared with eggs, in stuffing for birds, fish, &c. Quantities are exported to England, but more from the West Indies than the East. The price in London is from 15s. to 25s. per cwt. Of the various kinds, *C. baccatum*, bird's eye pepper, *C. fastigiatum*, cayenne pepper, *C. frutiscens*, Chili pepper, and *C. Nepalénse*, Nepaulese pepper, are the best known. The following is the method in which cayenne pepper is made by the natives from capsicums: They dry the ripe fruits in the sun, and then in an oven in an earthenware pot, with flour put between the layers of fruit. When quite dry they are cleaned from the flour and pounded to powder. To this is added flour in the proportion of a pound of wheat flour to every ounce of pepper, and the mixture is made up into cakes with leaven. These are baked until as hard as a biscuit, then beaten again into a powder and sifted. In this state the pepper is ready, after being packed in tin cases, and soldered down to exclude the air, for exportation.

In preparing red pepper for ourselves from the capsicums grown in our own garden, we simply dried them first of all in the sun, re-dried them in the oven (or, at least, the khánsámán did), and they were then pounded and sifted for use.

Radishes (Hindustani, *moollee*) we grew in quantities, sowing the seed broadcast in small beds from June to February; it is trodden in, and then the beds watered. When the plants are about 3in. high they should be well thinned, leaving about 4in. or more between each plant. In from four to six weeks they will be fit to pull. The country radishes are fairly good; but those grown from imported seeds have more flavour.

Leeks, known as *Belatee Peeaj*, are sown broadcast in beds from July to August, transplanted when about 6in. high into rows, and set about 12in. apart. They do well in most parts of India, more especially in the Deccan.

In the preceding remarks I have dwelt more particularly on the English vegetables with which we are all acquainted, and the method of treating them when grown in India; but there are very many native vegetables which deserve mention. I will name a few of those most used: There are various sorts of country beans, called collectively *saem*, such as the *balka* (garden bean), *balkazun* (kidney bean), both cultivated as the kidney bean would be, and cooked in the same ways; also the *bullur*, the *kulaee*, and the *kutt'hee* (horse bean). *Bheendee* is a very commonly grown plant, met with everywhere; the long capsules are cooked when green, boiled whole or sliced, and are made into soup. It is, when thoroughly well cooked, an agreeable vegetable to eat. *Brinjals* I have already named, and the methods of cooking them.

Yams, such as the *Guranto Aloo* (the red sweet yam), and the *Gurany Lal* (purple yam), may well be grown, especially the former, as they make a change in the vegetables served at your table; the *Disocroeas* have all large tuberous roots, but some of them are much more eatable than others; of these *D. globosa* is, perhaps, the best. They are usually found in the forests, where they are dug up in the winter and brought into the bazaars by the natives for sale; they are easy to grow, and are cooked in the same way as potatoes, but are much sweeter and more insipid to the taste. A small yam, the *D. aculeata*, is thought a good deal of; the tubers are whiter than those of the other yams. Starch is made from the tubers of another sort of yam, the *D. fasifculata*. The sweet potato (*Convolvulus Batata*) is also cultivated in many gardens, as well as a tuber called by the natives *Choopree Aloo*, the botanical name of which I do not know. Both are good, especially the first named; they are cultivated exactly in the same way as potatoes.

Ginger is a native of India, and attains to great perfection in that country. Green ginger forms an ingredient in very many dishes. *Adruk*, the native name for the plant, is planted by division of the green root, usually before the rains commence. It is set in the same beds in which it is to remain, but does not flourish well unless the soil is really suited to it; it needs a great deal of water. The stalks dry off, but the roots are allowed to remain in the ground sometimes for two years, always one, before they are taken up. It is largely cultivated in India, doing best in red earth, tolerably moist and free from gravel. When the roots are taken up, if for white ginger, they are scalded, scraped, and dried; if for black ginger, they are merely scalded, not scraped. When first dug up the rhizomes are red inside. The preserved ginger sold in shops is made from the young roots dug up before they have remained very long in the ground—about four months. The chief enemies to these roots are worms; sometimes whole crops are ruined by them, and there is no certain remedy. To make preserved ginger from the young rhizomes, they are, when dug up, scalded, and washed thoroughly in cold water, the water being changed every day for four days, then pealed with great care. When this operation is over, they are put into jars, which are filled up with a weak syrup of sugar. This syrup is changed every third day for nine days, each time being made stronger until the last time, then the jars are tied down, and are ready for exportation or sale in the country, as the case may be. The Calicut ginger is said to be the best produced in India.

Turmeric in India is very much used in cooking, being an ingredient in curries, chutney, and so on. Its native name is *Huldee*. There are four species of the plant; the sort used for culinary purposes is planted, as is ginger, in the place in which it is to remain, dug up when ripe (that is in about a year), and dried.

Sorrel is very commonly grown—that is, *Hibiscus Sabdariffa*, the red sorrel. It was introduced through the West Indies from the Mauritius. It is easily grown, and if the soil suits it develops into a bush about 4ft. in height, so a good space should be allowed between the plants, at least 3ft., or even 4ft. The leaves are made into sauce; they are picked over—young ones should be chosen—and washed, then put into a stewpan with an ounce of butter, the pan being covered and set over a moderate fire for about ten minutes or a quarter of an hour; they are then rubbed through a sieve, and seasoned with nutmeg, pepper, salt, and sugar. The juice of a lemon is added, and sent hot to table. It is an excellent sauce to serve with quail, or any small birds, also with cutlets. The ripe fruit of this plant is used for tarts and made also into jellies.

I have now mentioned most of the best known native vegetables. There are many others, but I am not much aquainted with them.

You should certainly find room for a plot of *Boota*, as the natives term the Indian corn, known to botanists as *zea mays*, for it is very useful, and can be eaten dressed in various ways. The plant is really a native of South America, but has been introduced thence to Europe, Asia, East and West Indies, and Africa. It grows anywhere and needs very little attention. It is usual to sow it at the beginning of the rainy season, the ground being prepared for it in May by being dug up, and, if poor, enriched with a little manure as a top dressing. In India it grows very well, and the large fields cropped with it present a very pretty sight, as it is a gracefully growing plant; even the corner we devoted to it in our compound always looked pretty, and formed a pleasing bit of colour to rest the eyes on. Maize grows from 7ft. to 8ft. in height. As a cereal it is very valuable, because of its comparative freedom from disease—neither rust, blight, nor mildew affecting it—and its growth is so strong that heavy rain does not beat it down. Insects, in the first stages of its growth, and birds, as the grain ripens, are its worst enemies. I am glad to see from the returns of acreage (it is not necessary to enter into the statistics here) that the cultivation of maize is spreading very rapidly in India, and it has now become a very important crop. In Behar and Upper India this is especially the case. The produce of the grain to the acre is larger than almost any other cereal, it having been known to yield under thoroughly favourable circumstances as much as from four to five hundredfold.

The heads are dressed green, the leaves stripped off, the grain heads plunged into boiling water, and served on toast, with melted butter, or the young ears are roasted in the same way as they would be when ripe, until the grains are brown, and then sent to table wrapped up in a napkin to keep them hot, and butter and salt served with them.

Good soup is also made from the tender grain. After the grains have become quite ripe and hard they are used in many different ways—ground into meal, which is known as "hominy," and is made into cakes, puddings, and porridge. Cattle are exceedingly fond of maize, but it should be coarsely ground before being given as food to any animal, or the grains do not digest properly, and often, by swelling, in the case of feeding poultry, cause obstructions, with sometimes serious results. Besides being of use for food, the leaves of the plant yield a fibre which has been utilised, when spun, as flax, and, when reduced to a pulp, for a paper material.

Rice, the common food of all natives, is the cereal of India, though wheat is now, especially in the Punjab and North-western provinces, making considerable headway. *Oryza sativa* is, however, not usually grown in compounds of limited space, as it is so easily procurable anywhere in India, and so cheaply that it would be waste of time and space to cultivate it on a very small scale.

CHAPTER XVI.

INDIAN FRUITS AND CONSERVES.

Mangoes — Mango Preparations — Mangosteen — Dates — Date Conserve — The Fig — Fig Jam — Ficus Bengalensis — Ficus Elastica — Grapes — Grape Culture — Grape Jelly — The Banana — Nutritive Properties — Preparations — The Orange — Its Medicinal Qualities — Various Uses — The Cocoa-nut tree — Bhere Fruit — Jamoon, or Jamboul — The Guava — Guava Jelly — Peaches — Apricots — Apples — The Pear — Bread Fruit — The Leichee — The Loquat — The Pummelo — The Lemon — Lime Juice — Tamarinds — Tamarind Preserve — Tamarind Water — The Pomegranate — Pomegranate Water.

A GREAT quantity of fruit of different kinds is grown in India; but abundant though it is, the quality is too often inferior. I am forced to confess that, with a few honourable exceptions, I was disappointed in Indian fruit. There are oranges in plenty, but they have mostly thick skins and woolly interiors, devoid of juice; peaches, of which one can only say "what a goodly outside falsehood hath," for tempting though their exterior seems, they are often rotten at the core. The mangoes, dates, lichies, however, with some others, are really good. First of all must be ranked—

Mangoes.—Many people are very partial to them, and the Bombay mangoes are really good. The trees in Bombay bear two crops every year, but this is not the case with all mango trees. It is a tree easily propagated, either by seed—which, however, is the slowest method of raising—cuttings, or grafting. A mango graft may be applied at any season of the year; the stock needs to be kept continually moist; a graft tree, however, never grows as large as a seedling. The finest flavoured sorts grown in India, that is in Western India, are the Doriah, Malgrobah, Raspberry, Mazagon, and Alphonso. The Malgrobah is the largest of all, and ripens the latest.

The culture of the mango (*mangifera Indica*) is easy, as it requires only a moderate degree of care. The tree is strengthened by being pruned, and in the cold weather the roots should be dug all round and old manure mixed with the soil. Seedlings take much longer to bear fruit than grafts, frequently not bearing until the sixth year, while those grafted bear, if allowed to do so, in the second or third year. The fruit is highly esteemed and is very wholesome, but the coarser sorts have a strong taste of turpentine. Unripe mangoes make good tarts, preserves, fool, and pickles. Iced mango fool, a recipe for which I gave in a former chapter, is an excellent dish in hot weather. Mangoes are preserved after this fashion: Choose some fine unripe mangoes, peel them, divide in half, and remove the seeds; the stones are cut in half and allowed to remain. Then to every pound of fruit allow $1\frac{1}{4}$lb. of sugar candy and one pint of water, put into a preserving pan and boil gently, stirring constantly, and skimming off all scum as it rises. Remove the pan from the fire when the mangoes look clear and are soft to the touch, let them stand in the pan till quite cold, then put into jars and tie down very carefully with brandied paper.

Mango Jelly is very good made thus: Peel some unripe mangoes and cut into slices, remove the stones, put the slices into a stew or preserving pan, with enough water to cover them, boil them gently until perfectly soft, then run through a jelly bag. To every pint of juice add $1\frac{1}{2}$lb. white sugar pounded fine; when it is all dissolved, put it into the preserving pan again and boil gently, constantly skimming and stirring the whole time. When it is fine, clear, and the scum ceases to rise, pour it off while warm into pots, and tie down very carefully.

Mango pickle.—Procure fifty fine mangoes (unripe), peel them and partly divide them through the shell, so as to remove the kernel from the inside. Strew salt thickly over them, and let them remain in a large tub for twenty-four hours. Make the following pickle: $1\frac{1}{2}$ pints of vinegar, 2oz. of turmeric; simmer this for a quarter of an hour, then take off the fire; add to the mangoes $\frac{1}{2}$ seer of dry chillies, $\frac{1}{2}$ seer of green ginger sliced, $\frac{1}{4}$lb. of mustard seed, free from husk, and 2oz. of garlic. Stuff the insides of the mangoes with these ingredients, which should also be thoroughly incorporated with them; stir them round until they are perfectly mixed together, then pour over the vinegar and turmeric. Before mixing up in this manner, the mangoes should have been removed from the tub into the jar in which it is intended to keep them. If the vinegar is not enough to cover the fruit, more must be added, and the jar very securely tied down. Mangoes are often dried in the sun in this way: the unripe fruit is taken, peeled, and cut into slices; these are well sprinkled over with salt and set in the sun to dry. They are then rolled into balls and hung in some dry place until wanted for use. Another plan is to boil the green mangoes with a little water until they are quite smooth; the pulp obtained from them is then dried in the sun, and when ready stored away in a dry place; when wanted for use a piece is cut off and soaked in water.

Mango Chutney (sweet).—Take a pound of mangoes—eight large mangoes when peeled and sliced are reckoned to the English pound—peel them and cut them into very small bits, chop up very small 2oz. green ginger, 2oz. garlic, 8oz. dried chillies, ground and mixed with vinegar, 8oz. sugar, and 8oz. salt, mix the mangoes well up with the other ingredients, put all into a jar and cork or tie it down very tightly; keep it out in the sun for a fortnight, and sometimes stir the chutney up well. A fresh and simple dinner chutney for immediate use can be made by peeling one green mango, and chopping it up into tiny pieces, adding one onion and three green chillies, cut up finely, a teaspoonful of salt and one of vinegar.

Mango Chutney (Colonel Skinner's recipe).—12oz. dried mangoes, 4oz. garlic, 8oz. each of ginger, salt, jaggery, and stoned raisins, 2oz. dried chillies, two and a half bottles of vinegar, the whole to be well ground down together, put into a well closed jar, and left out in the sun for a fortnight, when it will be fit for use.

Mango Sauce (Dr. Riddell's recipe).—1lb. each of green mangoes, salt, sugar, raisins, $\frac{1}{2}$lb. red chillies and garlic mixed, green ginger $\frac{1}{2}$lb., vinegar three quarts, lime juice one pint. Pound the first ingredients well, then add the chillies, garlic, and ginger, mix and expose them to the sun for a month, then strain through a piece of cloth, gently pressing the liquid; bottle off and cork down tightly for use. The sediment left after the straining is an excellent chutney.

I have devoted some space to mangoes because, in the estimation of many, they are the best fruit produced in India. The kernels of the nut contain a considerable degree of nourishment, but are not often used, except in times of famine, when the poorer natives boil and eat them. The pulp of a mango contains sugar, gum, citric acid, and gallic acid, the presence of which is shown by the blue stain left on a knife when a mango is cut with it.

Mango trees bear plentifully only under favourable circumstances, namely, a moist atmosphere. A mango famine, the natives say, foretells a grain famine, light rains, but healthy weather; mangoes in excess foretell heavy rains and plagues. If mangoes ripen before rain falls it is thought dangerous to eat them, which accounts for the following native saying, "Eat a mango before it rains and dig your grave."

Mangosteen (*Garcinia purpurea*) bears a fruit about the size of a small orange, of a deep purple colour; the seeds yield an oil known as kokum oil, which is an excellent application for chapped skin, scratches, &c. The fruit is very good, having an agreeable acid flavour, and is much used in jellies and syrups, and also eaten in its natural state. There are several trees in Bombay; they are handsome, growing to about 30ft. in height, with drooping branches, and lanceolar, shining dark green leaves, the fruit is smooth, brown outside, and, as before mentioned, purple within, the seeds also being of that colour. It grows in the Concans, in the ravines at Kandalla, and along the Malabar coast.

The true *mangosteen* (the *G. magostana*) is not a native of India, but was introduced from Singapore into Bombay. The fruit does not, moreover, attain to that perfection it does in the countries to which it is indigenous. The white pulp surrounding the seeds is most delicious, and has been likened to "perfumed snow." It is a pity that it does not succeed better in India, as it is the most wonderfully fine flavoured fruit, but neither in size nor in taste do the fruits resemble those produced from the trees in the Eastern Archipelago. The *G. pedunculata* also produces an edible fruit, which ripens in April or May. It is of large size, sometimes weighing as much as 2lb., and of a very acid flavour, but pleasant. Natives use it in curries, and for acidulating water. Cut into slices and dried in the sun it retains its acid qualities for years, and has much the same properties as a lime.

Dates, the fruit of the date palm (*phœnix dactylifera*), grow to great perfection in some parts of India. Mooltan, where we were for some time stationed, is famous for its date palms. They form a great feature in the landscape, and the fruit freshly plucked from the tree is, to my mind, one of the best of the various Indian fruits. It is a handsome tree, this date palm, shooting up in one cylindrical column, to the height of 50ft. or 60ft. without any division or branches, and is about the same thickness throughout its length. It throws out, at its extreme top, a splendid crown of leaves, which fall very gracefully; the chief stems of these leaves are, some of them, as long as 12ft.; they taper off at the end, and have the appearance of a gigantic fern. The bottoms of the leaves are enveloped in a sort of membraneous sheath; they are pinnated, each leaf being composed of a quantity of long and narrow leaflets; these are alternate, and bright green in colour. The flowers come out in large bunches or spikes from between the leaves. The tree is diœcious, the male flowers being on one plant, and the female, or fruiting ones, on another; the former are the largest. The stamens of the female flowers are tiny dates, not much bigger than peas. These swell until they attain their full size, the flowers withering off.

Dates are gathered for preserving a little before they are ripe, but if wanted for eating fresh they are left on the tree until they have perfectly ripened, in which state they are most excellent. They cannot, however, be kept in their ripe state for any length of time, or be sent to any great distance, as they soon ferment and become acid. This is why they are never tasted to perfection except in Eastern countries. Those intended for exportation are dried in the sun on mats. The dates which come into the European markets from Barbary and the Levant are always in this state; they contain a large amount of nourishment, and the Arabs rarely travel without a bag of them in the dried state.

Date Paste is prepared by pressing the fruit after the stones are extracted. The date palm is useful in many ways—the fruit for drying, pressing, and preserving, also for making into tarts. The stalks of the fruit and the kernels, by boiling, become quite soft, and cattle are fed on them. A strong spirit is distilled from the fruit. Palm wine is made from the sap of the tree. Only those trees which no longer bear fruit are cut down for this purpose. The fibrous parts of the leaves and stalks of the fruit are made into baskets, ropes, and mats. Cordage is made from the inner bark of the tree, and the trunk answers admirably for posts, rails, fencing, &c., because it is impervious to the attacks of white ants.

Another sort of date palm grows also in India, a smaller kind, the *Phœnix farinifera*. This is a lower growing tree, more bushy, and the leaves are greener. It flowers and fruits in much the same way, only the dates are almost black in colour when ripe, have not so much pulp, and are less pleasant to the taste, being more mealy and rather insipid. A farinaceous matter is obtained from the trunk, which by the natives is used for food.

The fig tree flourishes in India, and bears fruit almost all the year round. Two varieties are cultivated, the white and the blue; the best and finest fruit is borne by the young trees, from two to six years old.

In India the fig is called *unjeer:* it is easily grown, cuttings striking very readily in about six weeks. Manuring round the roots as the tree increases in size is much resorted to; old branches, as they have borne fruit, are pruned away each year, leaving a few buds to throw out healthy young shoots. There is something very curious about the fructification of the *unjeer*. The fig itself consists of a pulp containing a quantity of seedlike pericarps enclosed in a rind. The tree has no visible flower; the fruit rises at once from the joints of the tree in the shape of tiny buds, with a small perforation at the end; there is, however, no appearance of petals, but as the fig enlarges the flower comes to maturity in its concealment. In France and Italy the fruit is pricked as soon as it commences to ripen, and a drop of sweet oil is put on the spot, which is said to very much increase its size. I do not remember to have heard of this being done by the natives of India; but they protect it from the attacks of birds and insects by enclosing each fig in a muslin bag.

Fig Jam is often made in India. It is rather too luscious for my taste, but many are very partial to it. The ripe fruit is collected, carefully picked over, and skinned, then laid in a china bowl with sugar candy (pounded) strewed thickly over it. It should remain for twelve hours and then be weighed (allowing to each pound of fruit a pound of preserving sugar), be placed in a preserving pan, and be skimmed frequently until it is clear and begins to jelly, when it should be poured into pots, tying down when cold and firm.

The *Ficus Bengalensis*, or common banyan-tree, is nearly allied to the *Ficus carica*, being, indeed, called the Indian fig-tree, and it deserves notice, not on account of its fruit, but because it is a sacred tree, and held in immense veneration by the Hindoos. It attains a vast size and grows in a very singular manner, shooting down in the direction of the earth and taking root, until at last one tree forms a perfect grove, for as the rootlets attain maturity they, too, throw down their shoots, propagating in the same manner.

The *Ficus elastica* (Indian caoutchouc tree) comes under the same species, as do the *Ficus Benjamina, F. religiosa, F. racemosa, F. excelsa, F. oppositi folia*, and *F. rubescens*. Nearly all these have medicinal properties, and are used by the natives in various diseases; the bark, seeds, leaves, &c., being severally useful.

Grapes (in Hindustani *ungoor*), are cultivated nearly all over India; the finest come from the Deccan, with the exception of the Cabuli grape, imported from Cabul, of which I shall have occasion to write presently. The four sorts best known amongst the natives are the *Hubshe, Bokerie*, or *Abba, Fukkrie*, and *Sahiba*.

The general mode of culture is from slips, which are taken when the first cutting is over after the rains. When these slips are ready to be removed they are planted from 8ft. to 9ft. apart, and for the first year they are trained on dry sticks; then large straight branches of the *pangrah* are cut, a fork being left at the top of each branch to support the vine. These poles are stuck into the ground about a foot or so from the vine, if too far off it acquires a bend which is hurtful to it, for its stem cannot be too straight. The *pangrah* branches are usually 5ft. in height. It has been proved that the best soil in which to grow vines is that the natives call *pandree*, and is the white earth they build their houses of. In black soil, or even in a mixture of black and white, the grapes do not acquire so rich a flavour as they do in pandree, though in the mixture the vines themselves grow well, but they go to leaf too much, and the fruit suffers in consequence. It is usual to water the vines every third or fourth day during the hot and cold seasons after they have been cut for the first crop, which cutting takes place in April. The bunches require trimming as soon as they are about the size of small peas. When they are full and ripe, water must be withheld, unless in very dry soils. Directly the first crop is over the cutting for the second commences, unless it is thought advisable to check it, when the flowers should all be picked off as they appear. Most *mallees*, however, allow a second crop, as then the vine does not grow too luxuriantly, and so become weak. The vine roots are opened up after each crop, manured, and well watered. Dr. Riddell says that after the rains, when the vine is cut for the sweet crop, some gardeners pursue this method of treatment, which is considered, he adds, almost a secret: "2lb. of dried fish, 4oz. of common salt, and ½oz. of asafœtida are mixed up in sixteen quarts of butter-milk, and allowed to digest for three weeks. This quantity is sufficient for five trees. The vine is first cleaned of all its rugged and rough bark, which harbours insects, the leaves having been picked off about three weeks previous to cutting, with a view to hardening the wood; the vine is then cut, leaving three or four eyes only on each bough close to the stem. It is then allowed to drop four days, after which the earth is opened round the roots and cleared away. It remains in this state four days more; then the earth is again put round the roots mixed with a proportion of the above compost. The vine is left for another three days, when water is given to it. After this the watering ceases, until it is in full blossom, when irrigation is continued every fourth day during the season." The vines in the public gardens in India, the "company *baghs*," often form a very pretty sight, being grown in bowers and archways; the tree lends itself to this plan, being such a graceful free grower. It requires, however, plenty of sun and a certain amount of protection from wind, especially that from the north-west. Vine culture is making rapid strides in Cashmere, and it seems that before long India may be in a position to supply herself with wine of home manufacture, as she does with beer. Cashmere has long been the home, the Happy Valley in particular, of splendid grapes. At last the Maharaja appears to have had his eyes opened to the fact that a profitable industry may be made out of the grapes grown in his dominions. Three Frenchmen, trained experts in vine culture, now reside in the country—at Srinuggur—and all is being done that is possible to start the experiment well. Cuttings and seeds were imported from France some two or three years ago from the best French vines, and it is reported that these have thriven even beyond expectation. There is no reason to doubt that in time the wine from Cashmere will find favour not only in India, but in other countries, for the district is evidently well suited to the growth of the vine. The Cabuli grapes, to which I have before referred, are very generally eaten in all parts of India; they are very thick skinned, but have the true Muscat flavour. The traders bring them down country wrapped singly in cotton wool in boxes, in which state they travel very well.

The small sweet water grape makes a very good jelly, treated in the following manner: Pluck the fruit when quite ripe, put it into a stone jar, and stand the jar in a saucepan three parts full of cold water. Wrap the jar in hay or straw so that it does not move about; simmer for half an hour. Take it out and empty it into a jelly-bag. Strain the juice twice over, but do not squeeze the fruit at all. To every pint of juice add 1½lb. of loaf sugar; put it into a preserving pan and serve for nearly an hour, stirring and skimming all the time. When it is quite clear pour into jars and tie down very carefully with brandied paper.

This plan might well be tried at home with grapes that will not ripen fully, only in that case more sugar would have to be used.

The banana, or common plantain, the botanical name of which is *Musa paradisiaca*, is largely cultivated in India, and is very highly esteemed by the natives on account of its usefulness. It is common to both the East and West Indies, and several varieties are grown. In the Himalayas it flourishes at an altitude of 5000ft., and in the Neilgherries is found at the height of 7000ft. According to Lindley, there are ten species of musa, but it is not necessary to mention them all. The one under notice is that most generally met with. It is an herbaceous plant, with a simple stem thickly clothed with the sheathing petioles of the leaves, which form a large tuft at the top of the stem; the flowers grow in spikes, and are of a yellowish white colour; in form the fruit is oblong, fleshy, with numerous seeds buried in pulp. It flowers all the year round, and in eight or nine months after the sucker has been planted the fruit begins to form in clusters, which are fit to cut in the tenth and eleventh months. When the stalk is cut, the fruit of which has ripened, a sprout is put forth, and this bears fruit again in about three months. This second crop is not, however, of such good quality as the first, and is very frequently cut down, the surrounding shoots springing from the base of the stem being allowed to blossom and bear instead. It is usual to grow the plants in clusters or beds in a rich soil; and those so treated bear very fine fruit. They need little attention; the labour required for a plantation of bananas is to cut the stalks which are laden with fruit—they are cut before being quite ripe, when they are seen to change colour, and hung up to ripen in the house—and give manure round the roots, digging up the earth and mixing the manure with it twice a year. One cluster of bananas, produced on a single plant, often contains from 150 to 170, and weighs from 50lb. to 70lb.

The banana is considered most nutritious and very wholesome, either cooked or eaten in its natural state, and is so easily grown that the natives have usually a small plantation of plantains round their huts. In many parts they nearly live on them, and so highly do they esteem the plant that during their numerous festivals, or on the occasion of a marriage, this emblem of plenty and fertility will be seen placed at the entrance to the house. It grows well in almost any soil, provided it is nourished fairly; manure, every year or twice a year, is essential to its well being. Newly-cleared forest land is said to suit it best where the soil is enriched with decayed vegetable matter. If the stem which has borne fruit is cut down when the fruit has been gathered, new shoots spring up very quickly round the old stem, and as these are cut others shoot up in their places, and will continue to do so from fifteen to twenty years in succession. The fruit is so nutritious that Professor Johnston wrote of it in the *Journal of the Agricultural Society of Scotland:* "We find the plantain *fruit* to approach most nearly in composition and nutritive value to the potato, and the plantain *meal* to those of rice. Thus, the fruit of the plantain gives 37 per cent. and the potato 25 per cent. of dry matter." It contains alkaline matter, potash, and soda salts, as does the potato, and both possess nearly the same percentage of phosphoric acid and magnesia. As far, therefore, as the supply of the mineral ingredients are concerned, the plantain, or banana, equally with the potato, is fitted to sustain the physical strength.

The ripe fruit of the banana is preserved by drying in the sun, and these dried bananas are pleasant and agreeable to the taste. They form an article of commerce in Bombay, and also in other parts of India. Meal is extracted from the fruit also by cutting it in slices, drying in the sun, and then pounding. It is to this meal Professor Johnston refers. Besides the uses of this fruit as food, the plantain, particularly the *Musa textilis,* yields a fibre which is a very good substitute for hemp, and the *musa* above mentioned likewise yields a very fine sort of flax, from which a delicate cloth is manufactured; the coarser kinds of fibre are useful for cordage, ships' ropes, and also for paper manufacture. Some very durable kinds of paper have been made in India from this fibre, and some also of fine quality. The leaves (young ones) are used in dressing blistered surfaces, and are very effectual in healing the same, also in dressing ulcers and wounds, while a water which flows from the stem of the plant has been found useful in cases of hemorrhage from the lungs, &c. The preserved (dried) fruit is a nourishing and antiscorbutic article of diet for long voyages. Green plantains are often made into chutney thus: Peel off the skins of three or four green plantains after they have been well roasted; grind up some *dhall*, about a tablespoonful, and three dried red chillies, and fry in butter; then pound altogether, adding salt and the juice of a green lime. As far as flavour is concerned, the small banana, supposed to be the real banana of the West Indies, is, perhaps, the best of all; some of the larger kinds are very insipid to European taste. Those we see in the shops here are cut in quite a green state, and ripened in the sun after they reach our shores; but their flavour gives you but a faint idea of the taste of one of the small luscious bananas which are picked off the plant almost ripe, and are ready to eat in a day or two at most. Fried bananas are very excellent, as also in puddings or tarts—in the latter with the addition of custard.

I used to amuse myself in India by trying experiments with the fruits of the country, sometimes with good results, and occasionally with the reverse. The oranges are, I think, the most disappointing of Indian fruits; they have, in most cases, such abnormally thick skins, such provokingly woolly interiors, and so little juice. I am writing now of the large common sorts. The finest kinds are the Cintra (these have a thin rind), the Cowlah, and the Mandarin (I think it is called), a tiny orange, but deliciously sweet. There is a large Mandarin orange with a very loose skin, and I conclude the smaller is of the same kind, as the skin is loose and comes off very easily, the fruit within being sweet-scented and juicy. It is the common orange of the country, called *koda* by the natives, which is such a very indifferent product. The Sautgur oranges are good, as are the *Burrachin* or large China; but these are from imported seed— at least, the latter is. The chief method of culture is by budding, the stocks being generally seedlings or cuttings from the sweet lime; the operation of budding is best performed in the cold season. There are very many ways of preserving and cooking oranges, and most of the methods in vogue in England obtain in India—for example, orange puffs, orange cheesecakes, orange custard, orange tart, orange fool, orange fritters, orange jelly, orange chips, candied orange peel, orange syrup, *compôte* of oranges, oranges *glacés*, oranges preserved whole, in syrup, in wine; marmalade, &c. The Indian oranges — that is, the inferior sort—are much better prepared in some way before eating, and there are so many ways of dressing them that no difficulty need arise on that score. The Hindoos have a strong belief in the medicinal properties of oranges as purifiers of the blood, and in this I quite agree with them, for I firmly believe that if people would take, habitually, an orange *au naturel*, either the last thing at night or the first thing in the morning, they would find their health in many ways improved by the practice. The rind, it is well known, is a useful carminative, and a very valuable addition to bitter infusions in cases of dyspepsia. Pulverised and added to rhubarb and magnesia, the rind is given in cases of gout. The fruit itself (ripe) is invaluable in scurvy, and the pulp roasted is used as an application to ulcers. Orange water is used in medicine, in cooking, and as a perfume, the flowers being distilled for this purpose; in fact, there are a hundred and one ways in which the fruit of the *Citrus aurantium* is useful to mankind. I have forgotten to name the orange as an ornamental plant in our greenhouses, but certainly this might also be mentioned when summing up its many uses. I have at this present moment in my mind's eye a large orangery which I walked through not long since—three greenhouses turned into one large one, opening out of a library in a country house, the whole forming a pleasant walk for its aged owner. The orange trees when I was there were in their full beauty, the houses heavy with the scent of their flowers, and from beneath their glossy dark green leaves peeped the fruit in all its stages of growth, green and tiny as well as fairly large and deep yellow, or rather, orange-coloured, the snowy flowers adding not a little to the beauty of the houses. Some of these trees are very old, and I remember them well in my childhood. Now they are tall and spreading, reaching high above my head; some of them must be from 18ft. to 20ft. or more, presenting a unique sight in England, and reminding one of orange groves abroad.

The cocoa-nut tree (*Cocus nucifera*) is so well known that it is hardly necessary to describe it. Its usefulness it is scarcely possible to over-rate; its roots are chewed by the natives, its young buds are cooked as a vegetable and eaten, the juice from its stems is made into palm wine, and also toddy, from which the fiery arrack is distilled. The ripe fruit is very good for food; the bark forms a very valuable fibre—the coir of commerce; the leaves are used for thatching the native huts, and they are also made into baskets, hats, lanterns, buckets, brushes, and fans; their ashes, when burnt, yield potash; the shells of the nuts are made into drinking cups. The kernels yield on pressure the cocoanut oil so much in demand, and candles are made from the refuse left from oil making. This oil is much used in India for lamps and also for culinary purposes. Each tree bears from eighty to 100 nuts, and continues bearing for over 70 years. It grows to the height of from 60ft. to 90ft., the leaves measuring from 12ft. to 15ft. in length. Cocoa-nut trees grow best near the sea; but they also flourish inland, and, indeed, thrive readily anywhere when cultivated. For the first few years they need care and watering, after which they grow very well of themselves with little or no attention. The cocoanut palm was introduced into India from Ceylon, since when its cultivation has steadily increased. A considerable trade is done in cocoa-nut oil, which is exported in large quantities from Bengal, Bombay, and Madras to other countries, England taking a large share of the exports. The oil fetches, generally, from £40 to £50 per ton, but sometimes a good deal more.

Bhere Fruit (*Ziziphus Jujuba*) is common all over India, the tree which bears it being found in nearly every jungle. It has a pleasant flavour, and ten crops are obtained each year, the best being that plucked in January. In shape the fruit is oblong, and it contains a stone; the taste rather resembles that of a fresh apple.

Jamoon or *Jambool*, known by botanists as *Eugenia Jambolania*, is a large and very handsome tree, bearing a fruit very much like a common blue plum, which is generally soaked in salt and water before it is eaten to lessen its roughness to the taste. It makes a very good jelly prepared thus: The fruit, after washing, is boiled with a little water until very soft, strained, then lime juice is added, and it is re-boiled, being reduced very much in the second boiling. Sugar candy is then added in the proportion of $1\frac{1}{2}$lb. to 1 pint of juice. When it sets well, it is allowed to partially cool, and then poured into pots and tied down. It is a beautiful colour when ready, a rich deep purple, and very good to the taste.

The Guava.—This tree grows nearly all over India. The fruit is unpleasant to eat in its natural state, as it has such a very powerful and disagreeable smell. If kept when ripe in the house the odour is simply unbearable, but made into jelly it is delicious, as most people are well aware; it is also made into preserve. The following is a good recipe for making

Guava Jelly.—Take 8lb. of ripe guavas, peel them carefully, and divide them into quarters; boil them with a little water, and strain through a jelly bag; then add the juice of eight limes, or ten if small, and $1\frac{1}{2}$ lb. of sugar candy; boil again, and skim very frequently until it is ready to set. Test it on a plate to see if it sets readily; then, if jars are used, pour hot into them, but if glass bottles, allow to partially cool before pouring off. Tie down securely.

Peaches grow fairly well in India, but the fruit is mostly of an inferior description. Some, however, that I have tasted were of good flavour, but they, though they look nice outside, are too frequently rotten at the core. They are easily cultivated after much the same manner as in England, well pruned, kept watered, and the insects which infest them kept down. As the fruit ripens it must be enclosed in bags to prevent birds and insects attacking it.

Apricots are not grown to much perfection in India, the fruit not ripening well.

Apples, English and Persian, grow well in the Deccan and in other parts; they are treated in the same way as in England. The "borer," a sort of caterpillar, is very destructive to them, and must be carefully looked for and destroyed.

Pear Trees are rare, and the fruit of a very coarse description, hardly fit even for stewing.

The Alligator Pear, known as *Laurus Persea*, and called very often "subaltern's butter"—why I do not know—is a very peculiar fruit. The tree which bears it is of a large size, and the fruit itself is from six to seven or eight inches long and about three inches thick. The outside skin is dark green; the interior is a white creamy sort of pulp, rather sweet to the taste.

The Bread-Fruit Tree bears another curious fruit, the size of a large orange; it is usually cut into slices and fried as potatoes would be, and the taste is not unlike that of a sweet potato.

It ripens best in the Deccan, the fruit on the large Bombay trees rarely attaining perfection.

The Leichee was introduced originally from China. It is a large tree, an evergreen, and the fruit is dark brown in colour, the inside pulp being yellow, glutinous, and sweet to the taste; but its quality is very inferior to that of the Chinese fruit. March and April are the months in which it is ripe and fit to eat.

The Loquat, called botanically *Meopilus Eriobotryna Japonica*, is another fruit tree introduced from China. It bears two crops of fruit in the year, the latest being the best. In colour the loquat is yellow, has a thin skin, and contains a sweet pulp, which has an agreeable taste.

The Pummelo, or *Citrus Decumana*, is the largest of all the orange tribe. It is very ornamental, and is found in nearly every Indian garden. The fruit is very large, rather coarse, but much esteemed for preserving. Candied pummelo peel is much used in cooking. A liqueur is made also of the rind.

The *Lemon Tree*, called by the natives *Neemboo*, and by botanists *Citrus lemona*, grows all over India. There are a great many varieties, and most are very easily cultivated; the fruit of both large and small kinds yields a quantity of juice, from which most refreshing drinks are concocted. The lime, which is the smallest of the lemon tribe, is very productive, fruiting all the year round, if well looked after, carefully pruned, and watered.

The Sweet Lime is another variety, and is called in Hindustani *Meeta neemboo*. The juice of this fruit makes a very excellent beverage for invalids.

The simplest manner of making a lime juice drink is to cut the limes in halves, and squeeze them in a wooden lemon squeezer, straining the juice afterwards, and adding sugar to taste; it should be iced, which makes it much more refreshing, and should always be made from freshly gathered limes or lemons. Lemon whey is made by taking the strained juice of two lemons, adding to it a pint and a half of milk, simmering it with sugar (pounded white) added to taste, and then re-straining it carefully through muslin. Green limes are very largely used in India in cooking various dishes, and for ordinary use as a cooling drink, and in cases of fever. They are also preserved whole, or in portions; syrup is made of them, pickle, marmalade, jelly, and so on.

Tamarinds, the fruit of the *Tamarindus Indica*, are very

useful; the red tamarind is the most valued, but it is rather scarce. The pulp of the pods is used both in food and medicine. The juice is very pleasant, containing a larger proportion of acid with the saccharine matter than is usually found in acid fruit. Tamarinds are excellent preserved.

Tamarind Preserve.—Take off the outer shells and split the tamarinds lengthwise in order to remove the seeds; have four times the weight of the fruit of finely powdered sugar, and make into a syrup, boiling it thoroughly, and adding the juice of three, four, or more limes, according to the quantity of fruit used; this juice must be strained before putting to the syrup, then, after it has boiled a few minutes, put in the tamarinds; allow to simmer for about five minutes, then take off the fire, and put the fruit into jars, pouring the syrup over; cover down the jars. The fruit for preserving should be gathered just before it is ripe. Another and more simple way of preserving this fruit is to put it into jars, in alternate layers of fruit and powdered sugar until the jars are full. The jars should be of stone. So preserved, tamarinds keep their colour and their taste well.

Tamarind Water is a refreshing drink for invalids. It is made by removing the outer shells, splitting the tamarinds lengthwise, and pouring boiling water on the fruit, powdered sugar being added to taste. The jug must be covered over, and the liquid allowed to cool very gradually; it should be strained before use. In cases of fever it is a good drink for the patient, but as it is a slight laxative it must be given with a certain amount of caution. In sore throat both tamarind water and the pulp administered by itself are good. Sauce made from the fresh fruit is in India generally served with roast duck. The tamarind has also economic uses. The timber is hard and good for building purposes, and a yellow dye is obtained by infusing the leaves; it yields a red dye also. There is a considerable export trade in tamarinds from Bombay and Madras.

The Pomegranate Tree (*Punica Granatum*) is not a native of India, but is indigenous to Carthage, and was thence introduced into India, France, Barbary, and Southern Europe. Royle, however, says it grows wild in the Himalaya. The fruit is useful in medicine, the rind being chiefly employed. The pulp is a gentle laxative, and a refreshing drink is made from it. In cases of dysentery a decoction made from the fruit is often given with success.

Pomegranate Water is made in the same way as tamarind water.

The other Indian fruits do not call for much notice. The bilimbi, bullock's heart, cashew-nut, hog-plum, kurunder, olive, paneola plum, papaw, pistachio-nut, star apple, sapota, soursop, and wampee, are amongst those most frequently met with. Of European fruits cultivated in India, and hitherto not mentioned, are the berberry, strawberry, blackberry, raspberry, gooseberry, mulberry, white, red, and black, pineapple, common plum, quince, and walnut, all of which are grown in different parts of the country.

CHAPTER XVII.

LIVE STOCK.

Management of Horses—Stabling—Saddlery and Harness—The Carriage — Forage — Ailments of Horses—Various Breeds — Cows — Their Treatment — Working Bullocks — Goats—Sheep—Rabbits—Teal and Quail—Turkeys, Geese, and Ducks—Peafowl—Occupation and Interest Created by Live Stock.

My book would be incomplete without a few suggestions as to the management of live stock.

First in importance, naturally, I rank the stable. Stables in India are very unlike the well-built stables we are accustomed to in England, for generally mud huts are made to do duty for the horses, and most likely these huts will be in the same row as those belonging to the servants, and be very much like them, as far as that goes—four mud walls, with a thatched roof, an opening for a window, ditto for a door, and with very primitive draining provision.

It is not, however, a work of much time to make the so-called stable a rather less miserable abode—at all events, a trifle more healthy for its inmates. We had the windows enlarged in the two huts—we only kept two horses—and chics fitted to them, the flooring taken up and relaid, sloping towards the drains in the centre of the huts, bars put before the doors (or the openings which served for them), racks fixed, not above the horses' heads—a very objectionable plan of fixing them, and too often ruling even in England—but on a level with the troughs for gram (corn). The huts were then somewhat an imitation of a loose box.

The native grooms (*syces*) never use brushes or other ordinary stable appliances, their method being to rub the horses with their naked hand and arm, and it is unwise to interfere with this custom, as they keep a horse's coat in very fine condition by mere "elbow grease." Of course, the syces want looking after; they are lazy, as are the whole fraternity of grooms, white or coloured, requiring to be kept up to their work and to have a watchful eye over them, for too often they will steal the horses' grain, and in cold weather strip the animals under their charge of the clothing you have provided for them, wrapping themselves in it instead. A visit to your stable at night every now and then, and always at different hours, is quite necessary to detect these malpractices and stop them.

The native manner of tying up a horse (on the full stretch by heel ropes) is very bad, and should never be allowed, unless perhaps at night in the height of the hot season, and then only the hind legs should be fastened, but not tightly. To keep horses in good condition in India they must be exercised every day without fail. This exercise they generally get, as it is usual to ride or drive, as the case may be, twice every day—in the early morning and in the cool of the evening. Moreover, when a horse is brought home from his canter it is usual to walk him about until he cools before the hand rubbing is commenced.

All saddlery and harness is best kept in the bungalow in a spare room, as you can then look it over yourself daily and see that it is kept in thorough order, the steel bright and the leather soft and pliable. We always did this, the syces fetching the saddles and bridles from the house when they were required for use. A carriage would be kept in the vicinity of the stable, in one of the mud huts before mentioned. Covers should be provided for it, one of waterproof for the rainy season, and one of light washing material during the hot weather. Mats, whips, harness, and, in damp weather, cushions, should be kept in the bungalow. You must give an eye every now and then to the carriage itself, the wheels, linch-pins, pole, shafts, lamps, and so on, because you will not be told if they are in an unsafe condition, but left to find it out for yourself.

Keep the corn (gram as it is called in India) under lock and key, and give it out yourself. A large tin-lined box or grain chest, with a division, and a good padlock should be kept for this purpose; the box standing on bricks to allow a current of air to pass underneath, and prevent the contents getting damp or mildewed in the rainy season.

A horse is generally allowed about from 12lb. to 14lb. of grass per diem, besides his gram, averaging from 2 to 4 seers daily, according to the size of the animal and the amount of work he is required to do. The food should be varied now and then, urdawa being given alternately with gram and bran (*suthoo*) occasionally in mashes. Salt should be mixed with the food, and a bit of rock salt kept in the stable for the horse to lick—a large block, which there is no danger of his swallowing.

The "grasscut" (you have to keep one certainly, if not a couple, to look after two horses), goes out daily to cut the grass, returning with enough for a day's consumption. It is best, if possible, to get the grass cut fresh every day, as the horses eat it with more appetite. We made one grasscut do the cutting for two horses, but you cannot always depend on this; and in such case you would probably keep two syces; we had two, one for each horse. Grass bought in the bazaars, being generally stale, is not nearly so good as that your own men go out into the country and cut.

Every now and then you should give your cattle a spice ball; some give one a week; they tend to keep the animals in health and condition. It is best to get these from a good native "vet.," as they are cunningly made, and if you got a recipe and made them yourself you would not find them the same as those you buy from a native veterinary surgeon.

Your stable, with two horses, two syces, and one grasscut, ought not to cost you more than forty rupees a month, or about £4 English money; for this you would include three maunds, ten seers of gram, the same quantity of urdawa, two maunds of bran, four seers of salt, shoeing, wages, and, say, five or six rupees for incidental expenses, repairs, and so on. Thus you would reckon your yearly expenses at 480 rupees, or £48—I will call it £50. For that sum, with a little management, you ought to keep the stable in good order.

If the gram is bruised it will be found to go further, and is really better for the animals. If not bruised it should be soaked before being given, as the whole gram is apt to swell, and if such is the case it is very injurious to the animal eating it. It is a good plan to have your horses brought up in front of your bungalow, and see them fed yourself; if this be done, have the nosebags brought to you before being strapped on, as otherwise you may find them ingeniously stuffed at the bottom tightly with grass, and the corn, not of course the whole feed, some of which has been purloined, placed on the top.

Washing horses daily in the hot weather is a usual practice, and if the animals be thoroughly well dried, it is a beneficial one, but not else, and in the rainy season it should not be allowed, as they are very likely to get a chill from it. The amount of water must be regulated by circumstances, and, if possible, soft water should be given instead of hard. This, however, in India, is difficult to procure, so the water should be taken from the well some hours before it is required and allow to stand in the open air. This will soften it; or it may be drawn and thrown into a barrel without a cover, which has a tap fixed near the bottom, and drawn off. It must not stand too long, however, and if a cask is used in this way the water must frequently all be drawn off, and the inside thoroughly cleansed and scoured out. Horses keep their health in India pretty well; country breeds are very hardy and so are Arabs generally; English and Australian horses (walers) want care until they are acclimatised.

Country breeds are the best for all round work, and are not dear; for from £12 to £15 you may often pick up a very decent animal, which will be more useful than a high priced Arab. We had too excellent country breds which did all our work well, and never seemed sick or sorry. Horses suffer a good deal from "gripes" in India, and the more promptly they are treated when so attacked the better. Never let a horse suffering from this disease stand still; move him about briskly, and drench him as soon as possible with good gin. I have seen a whole bottle given in a bad case, and with great success. The animal should have its stomach hand-rubbed by two people, one on each side, briskly for a few minutes, then be walked about, then rubbed again, and so on, until the paroxysms seem to pass off, but the sooner the gin is given the better. Gripes are said to be brought on by drinking very cold water in large quantities when the animal is over-heated, but bad grass, or a sudden chill, will bring them on.

Horses in India are also very subject to sore backs. The best preventive—and we all know that "prevention is better than cure"—is to have a pad, called in India a *numdah*, cut to fit the animal's back beneath the saddle exactly. If this is always worn, the saddle—even that awkwardly-contrived thing, a lady's saddle—will not rub a horse. When the sores or blisters underneath saddles or harness are merely trifling, and are perceived at once, they should be bathed constantly with salt and water. If more serious, the following application will be found of service : Take a good-sized brinjal, or fruit of the egg plant (*Solanum melongena*), which is very generally grown all over India, boil it in arrack, then divide it in half, and soak it in the arrack. Apply the soft side, warm, to the sore every morning and evening, and relief will soon be given. You must look over your horses frequently, and also see to your saddles, if they or the harness require any attention, for a slight sore a native groom thinks of very little consequence, and he would not dream of telling the sahib or the mem-sahib about it.

Personal supervision, I would remark, all native servants require, whether indoor or outdoor, and this should always be borne in mind. With it they will make good servants, without it they will be lazy, and too often cheat to any extent.

Having disposed of the stables, I proceed to consider the care of cows, bullocks, goats, sheep, rabbits, fowls, and the like.

Of *cows*, the best for milch purposes are unquestionably the Guzerati, that is, in Western India; in the southern portion of the empire, the Mysore and Nellore; and in the upper provinces, the Nagore. The first named give the most milk, from five to six seers *per diem;* the others, Nellore and Nagore, about half that quantity; the usual time for calving is during the rainy season. Many people in India keep cows; indeed, if you want to have good butter, cream, and milk, you must do so.

In some parts there is a difficulty in obtaining good pasturage. The usual method is to send the animals out in the country under the charge of a milkman during the day, who brings them home to be milked at night, or else the cows are put in care of a herdsman, who is paid so much a head, from 4 to 8 annas a month, and he takes them out each morning, and brings them back in the evening. The amount of gram (corn) given to each cow depends on the amount of milk she is giving, but it is necessary to keep a very sharp eye on your milkman, or he will water the milk to increase the quantity, and when extra corn is allowed, take it for himself; and he is versed in every kind of artifice to deceive you. The price of good cows ranges from 30 to 80 rupees for a Guzerati, from 30 to 60 for a Nellore or Nagore, and from to 6 to 18 for a good country cow.

With regard to the making of butter, every pan, pail, &c., used must be kept even more scrupulously clean than in England, as the heat of the climate causes the milk to taint and turn sour very quickly. It must be strained through perfectly clean muslin into tin pans, or else those of glazed ware, not earthenware, this causing, from its porousness, an old scent, which even washing the pans cannot remove. The best pans are, really speaking, those large china ones which can be picked up very cheap in some bazaars; these should be fitted with fine screens to keep away the flies. If cream is wanted, it must be skimmed off before the milk has turned the least degree sour, which is very soon the case in India.

When the butter is taken from the churn as little water should be used in preparing it as possible, and it should be worked up with a wooden spatula, never touched with the hand. As I have already referred to butter-making in a former chapter, I need add nothing further here.

Working Bullocks are not very expensive animals to buy, unless they are well bred; but as an ordinary bullock does his work quite as well as one of a more choice description, it is really no gain to buy expensive beasts. They are fed on grass, cotton pods, boosah, and if worked very hard, should be allowed a little gram as well.

Goats are nearly always found where there are children, as the milk is supposed to be better and more nourishing for them than cows' milk. They are very easily kept, as they are not fastidious, but will eat almost anything. If, however, their milk is used for infants, then their diet must be checked and their food well looked after; a little gram should be given to milch goats every morning and evening, about 1lb., or less, at a time is sufficient; vegetable leaves, the outside cabbage leaves, tops of carrots, beet, and so forth are also very good, and easily obtainable if you have a garden. The animals must be tethered, and not allowed to run loose, as they are fearfully destructive, and if they get into a garden commit a great amount of damage. Where there are kids, and the mother is used as a milch goat, they must not be allowed to run with her all day, only at certain times, or if they are, they must be muzzled. The goats coming from the banks of the Jumna are excellent for milch purposes. They are rather a long-legged breed, however, and not nearly so handsome as the Surat goats, which are generally to be had in Bombay. These are a compact, short-legged kind, and are excellent milchers, giving, for a goat, a large quantity at a time.

Sheep are generally kept by regiments, and fed up—"gram-fed" that is; but private individuals are not often found keeping them, as in most stations there is what is called a "mutton club," of which I have written elsewhere. The Bengali sheep, when gram-fed, are capital eating. If the sheep are penned, the pens must be kept very clean; grain is usually given in the morning and evening; if they are driven out to feed they are fed before starting and again on their return in the evening; they are never left out at night for fear of wild animals, or driven out in the morning until the dew is off the ground, as it is very injurious to sheep. A little salt should always be given to gram-fed sheep; the amount of gram allowed to each animal averages usually about 1lb. *per diem*, but it is no use giving corn to any sheep until they have eight teeth in front. I have tasted wonderfully good mutton in India, gram-fed in this way, but we never kept the animals ourselves, belonging to a club, and having our mutton in turn with the other members.

Rabbits are kept in most compounds. Sometimes they give a good deal of trouble by burrowing, and getting out into the garden, where they commit sad havoc. Their hutches must be roomy, dry, and airy, and they must be well sheltered from sun and rain. The breeding hutches should be kept separate, and all compartments should be swept out and thoroughly well cleaned every day. The does should never be disturbed when they have littered, otherwise they will frequently eat their young ones, and they should be kept well supplied with fresh water. The young should be taken away from the dam when five or six weeks old, at which time it is usual to commence feeding them up for table. They should be kept apart in feeding hutches, and fed with great regularity. For food, give them cabbage and lettuce leaves, sliced carrots, wild endive, lucerne, jawaree, and bruised gram, just a little moistened. The bucks should have separate hutches, for if kept together they fight. Many people keep rabbits in a sort of artificial warren instead of in hutches. At one time we pursued the following method with ours: A large square hole was dug, about six or seven feet deep, and lined with bricks. This was filled up with earth, rammed down quite hard, and around it another wall was built, and covered in. In this the rabbits were put, and left to burrow as they liked, an opening being made leading into an enclosed yard, and a sliding door fixed; here their food was put. The rabbits can thus be chosen for killing. To my mind, however, the hutch plan is the best. The animals are more under view, and they create a degree of interest; moreover, a better check can be placed on their numbers, and they do not become so dirty as when allowed to burrow at will.

Teal and Quail are kept in pits underground, the former in light pits, the latter in the dark, because they fight so much. Two, three, or four pits, divided by sliding doors, are made, to allow of cleaning, the birds being driven from one pit to another while this operation goes on. Water is, of course, supplied, and the birds are fatted up with small grain of various kinds. We usually had about fifty teal and 200 quail, and kept up the number, re-stocking as we killed off. These birds are quite invaluable in the hot weather, when good meat cannot be procured. They soon put on flesh, and a good fat quail or teal, from your own stock, carefully dressed, is a dish no epicure would despise. Many people keep fowls. We did not, but they are very easily reared in India, only they are little or no profit, as the men who look after them steal the eggs and the corn, and often sell the former to you, when, in fact, they have come from your own hens. The rules for keeping poultry in England apply also in India. Perfect cleanliness, good feeding, and daily attention are equally necessary; rice, jawaree, grain, ground Indian corn made into a paste, house scraps, vegetables, fresh liver, bones, &c., are used for food, which should be frequently varied, as the fowls in that case eat with more appetite. Fattening fowls are generally served with a mixture of ground wheat, rice, jawaree, and bran, made into a paste moistened with warm water, and it is given little and often during the day, any food left after feeding being carefully removed. A little suet, chopped very fine, and green food (cabbage and lettuce) chopped small, should be given every now and again as a relish. Cramming I do not agree with, either at home or abroad, though I know it is often done. Milk for fattening fowls is a good drink instead of water, allowing water sometimes also, and before killing, congee water, made with rice, should be given instead of water or milk. In all cases when water is used it should be first boiled.

Turkeys, Geese, and Ducks are also reared with ease in India. English treatment answers for all. They should be fed fully three times daily, have plenty of fresh (boiled) water; the food, ground grain, jawaree, rice in husks, and for the geese and ducks, coarse boosah mixed with the jawaree, and moistened with buttermilk. Under this regimen they will do very well, provided they are always kept scrupulously clean. The turkeys, when young, require very delicate feeding.

Peafowl are kept too. When young, they are fed as young chickens; and, when grown, on various sorts of grain, as are fowls.

There is great interest in keeping all live stock in India. The time so often hangs heavily, that it is quite a relief to have a garden to walk in and give instructions about; a warren, teal and quail pits to visit, fowls to look after, and the larger animals—horses, cows, bullocks, and goats, to see to and arrange for. They make so many objects for a stroll round the compound in the mornings and evenings, and they prevent that feeling of utter misery and disgust of everything which is apt to creep at times over the most stout hearted and energetic sojourner in a foreign land.

If there is really something to do, something to see after, the average Englishman or woman is generally willing to be up and about the work, whatever it may be. If there is literally nothing to be done, simply a "folding of the hands to sleep," then slowly, but surely, with inactivity and idleness, come illness and disease. So, my friends, you who mean to visit India, or rather who have to spend some portion of your lives there, whether you like it or not, make up your minds not to give in to the climate for an instant—unless, of course, your health unfortunately gives way. To keep your body in good health, your mind must never be allowed to be idle, and you can employ it in very many ways by taking an intelligent interest in the country, in the natives, and in your own immediate surroundings. Cultivate, as much as possible, an interest in all around you, and you will find that interest a safety valve, a preventive in many cases of downright illness, and in nearly every case of that baneful feeling of *ennui*, from which, in India, so many people suffer.

ADVERTISEMENTS.

INDIAN OUTFIT.
No. 1 LIST.

		s.	d.		£	s.	d.
12	Cambric Chemises, trimmed Work … … … at	3	6	=	2	2	0
6	Cambric Chemises, trimmed Embroidery … ,,	6	9	,,	2	0	6
12	Cambric Night Dresses, trimmed Embroidery … ,,	5	6	,,	3	6	0
6	Fine Night Dresses, trimmed … … … … ,,	7	6	,,	2	5	0
12	Pairs Cambric Drawers, tucked … … … ,,	3	6	,,	2	2	0
6	Pairs Cambric Drawers, trimmed … … … ,,	5	6	,,	1	13	0
6	Longcloth Petticoats, tucked … … … … ,,	4	6	,,	1	7	0
3	Longcloth Petticoats, trimmed … … … ,,	8	6	,,	1	5	6
1	Longcloth Petticoat, trimmed … … … ,,	14	6	,,	0	14	6
6	Nainsook Muslin Camisoles … … … … ,,	4	6	,,	1	7	0
3	Fine Nainsook Camisoles … … … … ,,	6	6	,,	0	19	6
6	Gauze Merino Vests … … … … … ,,	3	6	,,	1	1	0
3	Flannel Petticoats … … … … … ,,	8	6	,,	1	5	6
1	Print Morning Wrapper … … … … ,,	15	6	,,	0	15	6
1	White Brilliante Wrapper … … … … ,,	21	0	,,	1	1	0
1	Flannel Robe de Chambre … … … … ,,	21	0	,,	1	1	0
1	Five o'Clock Tea Gown … … … … ,,	42	0	,,	2	2	0
1	Flannel Toilet Jacket … … … … ,,	10	6	,,	0	10	6
1	White Brilliante Toilet Jacket … … … ,,	10	6	,,	0	10	6
12	Pairs Lisle Thread Hose … … … … ,,	2	0	,,	1	4	0
6	Pairs Balbriggan Hose … … … … ,,	2	3	,,	0	13	6
12	Cambric Pocket Handkerchiefs … … … ,,	0	9	,,	0	9	0
12	Hemstitched Pocket Handkerchiefs … … ,,	0	10½	,,	0	10	6
1	Pair French Wove Corsets … … … … ,,	10	6	,,	0	10	6
2	Dozen Towels … … … … … … ,,	12	6	,,	1	5	0
6	Sets Linen Collars and Cuffs … … … ,,	1	9	,,	0	10	6
	Haberdashery—an assortment … … … …				0	10	0
					£33	2	0

The above Outfit can be had for the Colonies or any part of the world; and, if desired, any article can be had separately. The Night Dresses, if wished, can be had with short sleeves for warm climates.

CHEQUES CROSSED LONDON AND WESTMINSTER BANK ST. JAMES'S SQUARE.

MRS. ADDLEY BOURNE,
LADIES' OUTFITTER,
CORSET, AND BABY LINEN MANUFACTURER.
37, PICCADILLY (ST. JAMES'S CHURCH), LONDON.

INDEX.

A.

	PAGE
Aden	32
Agra	41
Alexandria	31
Allahabad	38
Amusements on the voyage	29
Anglo-Indian furniture sales	61

B.

	PAGE
Baggage, arrangement and disposal of	3
Charges for excess	2
Insurance of	19
Passengers embarking at Brindisi may have it conveyed from Southampton	2
Weight allowed on board	1
Bombay, the town, places of interest	34
Boots and shoes	14, 22
Bungalows	55
External appearance of	55
Ground plan of	56
Internal arranemgent of	57
Native landlords of	57
Precautions in hiring	57
Rent of	55
Water supply of	57
Butchers' meat	68

C.

	PAGE
Calls social	82
Cawnpore	39
Choice of food	68
Cholera, the	39
Confluence of the Jumna and the Ganges	39
Cows for milch purposes	135
Treatment of	135

D.

	PAGE
Dairy produce	76
Delhi boil, the	75
Diminution of salaries	66
Dinner parties	85
Attendance for	87
Dishes for	88
Dishes, various	77
Resources of native cooks for	85
Special menus for	85
Table decoration for	87
Duties, daily, in India	81

E.

	PAGE
Eating and drinking	70
English equivalents of Indian currency	66

F.

	PAGE
Fares to India...	2
Fare, variation of	70
Forage	132
Fruits and Conserves, Indian	114
Furnishing	59
Carpets	60
Catalogue of requirements in	62
Furniture and fittings	61
General domestic appointments	63
Hangings	60
Matting in	59
Prices of articles of furniture	62
Scinde rugs	60
White ants, their destructiveness, and the means of prevention	59

G.

Garden, the	96
Grass plots in	98
Hedging of	98
Irrigation of	96
Manures for	99
Native deficiences as to	99
Produce of	100
General augmentation of prices	65

H.

Hills, the	84
Horses	133
Ailments of	134
Cost of keeping	133
Hotels and charges	40
Hot season, the	84
Housekeeping	65
Cost of	65

I.

India, means of getting there	1
Daily duties in	81

	PAGE
India—*continued*.	
Fares to	2
Hot season in	84
Housekeeping in	65
Increase of luxury in	66
Live stock in	131
Night travelling in	41
Occupation and health in	84
Routes to	1
Servants in	45
Society in	81
Sport in	23
Voyage to	25
Indian fruits and conserves	114
Gardening	96
Hotels and charges	40
Outfits for gentlemen	20
Outfits for ladies	8
Outfits for the married	15
Parcels post	6
Railway travelling	35
Scenery	35, 43
Servants	45
Society	81
Sunset	41
Tea and coffee	76

J.

Jubbulpore	38

K.

Khedive's Palace, the	31
Kitchen expenses	68

L.

Lines of steamers to India the P. and O., the Bombay Anchor, the Clan, the Hall line, Calcutta Star, Rubatino	2
Live stock, management of	131
Luxury, increase of	66

M.

	PAGE
Malta	30
Marble Rocks, the	38
Marketing	68
Memorable well at Cawnpore	39
Menus	71
Miscellaneous stores	18
Mooltan	43
Morning meal, the Indian	73
Mutton clubs	68

N.

Native cooking	68

O.

Occupation and health	84
Off the port of Bombay	38
Outfit for gentlemen	20
Boots and shoes in	22
Clothing in	20
Dress and morning suits in	22
General remarks on	20
Packing of	23
Plate in	24
Saddlery in	23
Shooting and fishing equipment in	23
Stationery in	23
Toilet requisites in	23
Underclothing	21
Outfit for ladies	28
Boots and shoes in	14
Cost of	10
Dresses in	10
Hats and bonnets in	12
List of, commonly given, too extravagant	8
Miscellaneous requisites of	12
Personal linen in	8
Requirements of	9
Unmade materials in	11
Outfit for the married	15
Bed linen in	16

Outfit for the married—*continued.*

	PAGE
Coverings in	16
General household requisites	17
House linen in	15
Linen sheeting not included in	16
Materials for making up in	18
Miscellaneous stores in	18
Table linen in	17

P.

Packing	3
Of regimental baggage	5
Places en route	30
Port Said	32

R.

Railway travelling	35
Provisions for the journey	36
Red Sea, a trying portion of the voyage	1
Refreshments, in	35
Scenery by the way	35, 43
Requisites on board ship	3
Routes to India—overland—by the P. and O. steamers—*via* Southampton—*via* Brindisi	1

S.

Saddlery and harness	132
Servants	45
Characteristics of Indian	42
Complaints respecting	46
How to treat	52
Necessary precautions in engaging	45
Remarks on	51
Selection of	45
Variety of, and their respective duties	50
Wages of	49

	PAGE
Society	81
Agreeableness of Indian	83
Customs and observances of	81
Stabling	132
Stimulants warning against	74

T.

Tea and coffee, Indian	76
Tiffin	81

U.

Unfiltered water, danger from	75

V.

	PAGE
Visits	82
Voyage out	25
Amusements on	29
Places en route	30
Requisites on board ship on	26
Sea-sickness on	28
Season for sailing	25
Ship regulations on	28

W.

Weights and measures	67
Wines and other drinks	74

www.ingramcontent.com/pod-product-compliance
Lightning Source LLC
Chambersburg PA
CBHW030345170426
43202CB00010B/1244